mile-a-minute
AFGHANS

If you're hooked on the relaxing pace of mile-a-minute crochet, then you're going to love this new book! Mile-A-Minute Afghans is overflowing with projects for all skill levels and styles to please everyone — from soft wraps for baby to handsome creations for men. You'll also discover floral fancies, rustic wonders, classic beauties, and colorful cover-ups.

This invaluable collection of 56 timeless throws has lots of exciting new afghans by today's most popular crochet designers. There's a versatile selection of our favorite mile-a-minute throws from Leisure Arts publications, too.

With patterns so easy to do that you get the sensation of crocheting a "mile a minute," these afghans are all stitched in strips. Just start with a central foundation strip and add a border around it. The strips can be crocheted in little snippets of time found throughout the day, and they also make great take-along projects for crocheters on the go. You'll get such a satisfying feeling of accomplishment as you finish each piece!

Featuring simple-to-follow instructions that will keep you on track, Mile-A-Minute Afghans goes the distance to help you achieve winning results every time!

LEISURE ARTS, INC.
and
OXMOOR HOUSE, INC.

EDITORIAL STAFF

Vice President and Editor-in-Chief: Anne Van Wagner Childs
Executive Director: Sandra Graham Case
Editorial Director: Susan Frantz Wiles
Publications Director: Carla Bentley
Creative Art Director: Gloria Bearden
Senior Graphics Art Director: Melinda Stout

PRODUCTION
Managing Editor: Joan Gessner Beebe
Instructional Editors: Tammy Kreimeyer, Sarah J. Green, and
    Frances Moore-Kyle
Project Coordinator: Carol McElroy

EDITORIAL
Managing Editor: Linda L. Trimble
Associate Editor: Robyn Sheffield-Edwards
Assistant Editors: Tammi Williamson Bradley,
    Terri Leming Davidson, and Darla Burdette Kelsay
Copy Editor: Laura Lee Weland

ART
Book/Magazine Graphics Art Director: Diane M. Hugo
Senior Graphics Illustrator: M. Katherine Yancey
Photography Stylists: Christina Tiano Myers, Karen Smart Hall,
    Rhonda H. Hestir, Sondra Daniel, and Aurora Huston

BUSINESS STAFF

Publisher: Bruce Akin
Vice President, Finance: Tom Siebenmorgen
Vice President, Retail Sales: Thomas L. Carlisle
Retail Sales Director: Richard Tignor
Vice President, Retail Marketing: Pam Stebbins
Retail Marketing Director: Margaret Sweetin
Retail Customer Services Manager: Carolyn Pruss
General Merchandise Manager: Russ Barnett
Distribution Director: Ed M. Strackbein
Vice President, Marketing: Guy A. Crossley
Marketing Manager: Byron L. Taylor
Print Production Manager: Laura Lockhart

Mile-A-Minute Afghans
from the *Crochet Treasury* Series
Published by Leisure Arts, Inc., and Oxmoor House, Inc.

Library of Congress Catalog Number: 96-76035
Hardcover ISBN 0-8487-1532-2
Softcover ISBN 1-57486-043-7

TABLE OF CONTENTS

QUEEN ANNE'S LACE

*With its lacy panels of double and treble crochets, this
dreamy afghan is reminiscent of the wispy white wildflower.
A pretty picot edging finishes the timeless throw.*

Finished Size: 52" x 72"

MATERIALS
Worsted Weight Yarn:
  42 ounces, (1,190 grams, 2,880 yards)
  Crochet hook, size H (5.00 mm) **or** size needed for gauge

GAUGE: Each Strip = 4¹/2" wide
    8 rows = 4"

STRIP A (Make 5)

Ch 21 **loosely**.
Row 1 (Right side): Dc in fourth ch from hook **(3 skipped chs count as first dc)** and in next 4 chs, ch 3, tr in next ch, (skip next 2 chs, tr in next ch) twice, ch 3, dc in last 6 chs: 15 sts and 2 ch-3 sps.
Note: Loop a short piece of yarn around any stitch to mark Row 1 as **right** side and bottom edge.
Rows 2 and 3: Ch 3 **(counts as first dc, now and throughout)**, turn; dc in next 5 dc, ch 3, skip next ch-3 sp, sc in next 3 sts, ch 3, dc in last 6 dc.
Row 4: Ch 3, turn; dc in next 5 dc, tr in next sc, (ch 2, tr in next sc) twice, dc in last 6 dc: 15 sts and 2 ch-2 sps.
Row 5: Ch 3, turn; dc in next dc, ch 3, tr in next dc, skip next 2 dc, tr in next dc, skip next tr and next ch, tr in next ch, ch 3, dc in next tr, ch 3, tr in next ch, skip next ch and next tr, tr in next dc, skip next 2 dc, tr in next dc, ch 3, dc in last 2 dc: 11 sts and 4 ch-3 sps.
Rows 6 and 7: Ch 3, turn; ★ dc in next dc, ch 3, sc in next 3 sts, ch 3; repeat from ★ once **more**, dc in last 2 dc.
Row 8: Ch 3, turn; ★ dc in next dc, tr in next sc, (ch 2, tr in next sc) twice; repeat from ★ once **more**, dc in last 2 dc: 11 sts and 4 ch-2 sps.
Row 9: Ch 3, turn; dc in next 2 sts and in next 2 chs, dc in next tr, ch 3, tr in next ch, skip next ch and next tr, tr in next dc, skip next tr and next ch, tr in next ch, ch 3, dc in next tr and in next 2 chs, dc in last 3 sts: 15 sts and 2 ch-3 sps.
Rows 10-140: Repeat Rows 2-9, 16 times; then repeat Rows 2-4 once **more**: 15 sts and 2 ch-2 sps.
Finish off.

STRIP B (Make 4)

Ch 21 **loosely**.
Row 1 (Right side): Dc in fourth ch from hook **(3 skipped chs count as first dc)**, † ch 3, tr in next ch, (skip next 2 chs, tr in next ch) twice, ch 3 †, dc in next ch, repeat from † to † once, dc in last 2 chs: 11 sts and 4 ch-3 sps.
Note: Mark Row 1 as **right** side and bottom edge.
Rows 2 and 3: Ch 3, turn; ★ dc in next dc, ch 3, sc in next 3 sts, ch 3; repeat from ★ once **more**, dc in last 2 dc.
Row 4: Ch 3, turn; ★ dc in next dc, tr in next sc, (ch 2, tr in next sc) twice; repeat from ★ once **more**, dc in last 2 dc: 11 sts and 4 ch-2 sps.
Row 5: Ch 3, turn; dc in next 2 sts and in next 2 chs, dc in next tr, ch 3, tr in next ch, skip next ch and next tr, tr in next dc, skip next tr and next ch, tr in next ch, ch 3, dc in next tr and in next 2 chs, dc in last 3 sts: 15 sts and 2 ch-3 sps.
Rows 6 and 7: Ch 3, turn; dc in next 5 dc, ch 3, sc in next 3 sts, ch 3, dc in last 6 dc.
Row 8: Ch 3, turn; dc in next 5 dc, tr in next sc, (ch 2, tr in next sc) twice, dc in last 6 dc: 15 sts and 2 ch-2 sps.
Row 9: Ch 3, turn; dc in next st, ch 3, tr in next st, skip next 2 dc, tr in next dc, skip next tr and next ch, tr in next ch, ch 3, dc in next tr, ch 3, tr in next ch, skip next ch and next tr, tr in next dc, skip next 2 dc, tr in next dc, ch 3, dc in last 2 dc: 11 sts and 4 ch-3 sps.
Rows 10-140: Repeat Rows 2-9, 16 times; then repeat Rows 2-4 once **more**: 11 sts and 4 ch-2 sps.
Finish off.

Continued on page 6.

ASSEMBLY

Note: Lay out Strips beginning with Strip A and alternating Strips A and B throughout.

FIRST STRIP

To work **Picot,** slip st in third ch from hook.

With **right** side facing, join yarn with slip st in first dc on Row 140; † ch 5, work Picot, ch 2, ★ working in sts **and** in chs, skip next 2 sts, slip st in next st, ch 5, work Picot, ch 2; repeat from ★ 5 times **more** †; working in end of rows, skip first 2 rows, slip st in next row, ch 5, work Picot, ch 2, (skip next row, slip st in next row, ch 5, work Picot, ch 2) across to last row, skip last row; working in free loops of beginning ch **(Fig. 31b, page 124),** slip st in first ch, repeat from † to † once; working in end of rows, skip first row, slip st in next row, ch 5, work Picot, ch 2, (skip next row, slip st in next row, ch 5, work Picot, ch 2) across to last 2 rows; join with slip st to first slip st, finish off: 152 Picots.

REMAINING 8 STRIPS

With **right** side facing, join yarn with slip st in first dc on Row 140; ch 5, work Picot, ch 2, working in sts **and** in chs, (skip next 2 sts, slip st in next st, ch 5, work Picot, ch 2) 6 times, working in end of rows, skip first 2 rows, slip st in next row, ch 5, work Picot, ch 2, (skip next row, slip st in next row, ch 5, work Picot, ch 2) across to last row; working in free loops of beginning ch, slip st in first ch, ch 5, work Picot, (ch 2, skip next 2 chs, slip st in next ch, ch 5, work Picot) 6 times, ch 3, holding Strips with **wrong** sides together and bottom edges at the same end, slip st in corresponding Picot on **previous Strip (Fig. 28, page 122),** ch 3, skip first row on **new Strip,** slip st in next row, ch 3, slip st in next Picot on **previous Strip,** ch 3, ★ skip next row on **new Strip,** slip st in next row, ch 3, slip st in next Picot on **previous Strip,** ch 3; repeat from ★ across to last 2 rows on **new Strip,** skip last 2 rows; join with slip st to first slip st, finish off.

RUSTIC LAP ROBE

Worked in rustic colors, this handsome lap throw is an ideal gift for your favorite gentleman. Center strips of double crochet shells are bordered by double and single crochets to create the homey wrap.

Finished Size: 33" x 56"

MATERIALS

Worsted Weight Yarn:
  Tan - 13 ounces, (370 grams, 760 yards)
  Green - 13 ounces, (370 grams, 760 yards)
  Rust - 7 ounces, (200 grams, 410 yards)
Crochet hook, size J (6.00 mm) **or** size needed for gauge
Yarn needle

GAUGE: Rows 1-6 = 4"
        Each Strip = 3¹/4" wide

STRIP (Make 10)
CENTER

With Tan, ch 5 **loosely.**

Row 1 (Right side): 5 Dc in fourth ch from hook **(3 skipped chs count as first dc),** dc in last ch: 7 dc.

Note: Loop a short piece of yarn around any stitch to mark Row 1 as **right** side and bottom edge.

Rows 2-78: Ch 3 **(counts as first dc, now and throughout),** turn; skip next 2 dc, 5 dc in next dc, skip next 2 dc, dc in last dc.
Finish off.

BORDER

Rnd 1: With **right** side facing, join Green with slip st in center dc on Row 78; ch 3, (6 dc, ch 1, 7 dc) in same st; † working in end of rows, 3 dc in first row and in each row across †; (7 dc, ch 1, 7 dc) in free loop of ch at base of 5-dc group **(Fig. 31b, page 124),** repeat from † to † once; join with slip st to first dc, finish off: 496 dc.

Rnd 2: With **right** side facing and working in Back Loops Only **(Fig. 32, page 124),** join Rust with slip st in either ch-1 sp; ch 2, 4 hdc in same sp; † sc in next 9 dc, place marker around last sc made for joining placement, sc in each dc across to within 8 dc of next ch-1 sp, place marker around last sc made for joining placement, sc in next 8 dc †, 5 hdc in next ch-1 sp, repeat from † to † once; join with slip st to top of beginning ch-2, finish off.

ASSEMBLY

Place two Strips with **wrong** sides together and bottom edges at the same end. Using Rust and working in inside loops only, whipstitch Strips together, beginning in first marked sc and ending in next marked sc *(Fig. 33a, page 125)*.

Join remaining Strips in same manner, always working in same direction.

ROSY RIBBONS

A blanket of rosy hues, this cozy afghan is just the thing for cuddling up with your sweetheart. Rows of cluster stitches border the panels of fanciful shells on our truly romantic wrap.

Finished Size: 45" x 65"

MATERIALS
Worsted Weight Yarn:
 Rose - 29 ounces, (820 grams, 1,695 yards)
 Dk Rose - 28 ounces, (800 grams, 1,635 yards)
Crochet hook, size G (4.00 mm) **or** size needed for gauge

GAUGE: Each Strip = 7¹/₂" wide

STRIP (Make 6)
CENTER
With Dk Rose, ch 18 **loosely.**

Row 1 (Right side)**:** Dc in fourth ch from hook, ★ ch 3, skip next 2 chs, (sc, ch 2, sc) in next ch, ch 3, skip next 2 chs, dc in next 2 chs; repeat from ★ once **more**: 6 sps.

Note: Loop a short piece of yarn around any stitch to mark Row 1 as **right** side and bottom edge.

Row 2: Ch 1, turn; sc in first dc, ch 1, sc in next ch-3 sp, ch 3, skip next ch-2 sp, sc in next ch-3 sp, ch 2, sc in next ch-3 sp, ch 3, skip next ch-2 sp, sc in next ch-3 sp, ch 1, skip next dc, sc in top of beginning ch: 6 sc and 5 sps.

Row 3: Ch 1, turn; sc in first sc and in next ch-1 sp, 7 dc in next ch-3 sp, sc in next ch-2 sp, 7 dc in next ch-3 sp, sc in next ch-1 sp and in last sc: 19 sts.

Row 4: Ch 3 (**counts as first dc, now and throughout**), turn; dc in next sc, ch 3, skip next 3 dc, (sc, ch 2, sc) in next dc, ch 3, skip next 3 dc, 2 dc in next sc, ch 3, skip next 3 dc, (sc, ch 2, sc) in next dc, ch 3, skip next 3 dc, dc in last 2 sc: 6 sps.

Rows 5-159: Repeat Rows 2-4, 51 times; then repeat Rows 2 and 3 once **more.**
Finish off.

TRIM
FIRST SIDE
Row 1: With **right** side facing and working in end of rows, join Rose with slip st in first row; ch 1, work 235 sc evenly spaced across.

Row 2: Ch 1, turn; sc in each sc across.

Row 3: Ch 4 (**counts as first hdc plus ch 2, now and throughout**), turn; skip next sc, hdc in next sc, ★ ch 2, skip next sc, hdc in next sc; repeat from ★ across: 117 ch-2 sps.

To work **Cluster,** ★ YO, insert hook in sp indicated, YO and pull up a loop, YO and draw through 2 loops on hook; repeat from ★ 4 times **more**, YO and draw through all 6 loops on hook (*Figs. 17a & b, page 120*).

Row 4: Ch 2 (**counts as first hdc, now and throughout**), turn; ★ hdc in next ch-2 sp, ch 1, work Cluster in next ch-2 sp, ch 1; repeat from ★ across to last ch-2 sp, hdc in ch-2 sp and in last hdc: 58 Clusters.

Row 5: Ch 3, turn; dc in next hdc and in each ch-1 sp and each st across; finish off.

SECOND SIDE
Work same as First Side.

ASSEMBLY
Place two Strips with **right** sides together and bottom edges at the same end. Working through **both** loops of **both** pieces, join Dk Rose with slip st in first dc; ch 1, sc in same st and in each dc across; finish off.

Join remaining Strips in same manner, always working in same direction.

EDGING
TOP
Row 1: With **right** side facing, working in end of rows of Trim and in sts on Row 159, join Rose with slip st in first row; ch 1, work 183 sc evenly spaced across.

Row 2: Ch 1, turn; sc in each sc across.

Row 3: Ch 4, turn; skip next sc, hdc in next sc, ★ ch 2, skip next sc, hdc in next sc; repeat from ★ across: 91 ch-2 sps.

Row 4: Ch 2, turn; ★ hdc in next ch-2 sp, ch 1, work Cluster in next ch-2 sp, ch 1; repeat from ★ across to last ch-2 sp, hdc in ch-2 sp and in last hdc; finish off: 45 Clusters.

BOTTOM
Row 1: With **right** side facing, working in end of rows of Border and in free loops of beginning ch (*Fig. 31b, page 124*), join Rose with slip st in first row; ch 1, work 183 sc evenly spaced across.

Complete same as Top.

PEACHY TRELLIS

A pattern of front post treble stitches creates a trellis effect on this peach of an afghan. The texture is enhanced by working into the back loops of the border.

Finished Size: 46" x 70"

MATERIALS
Worsted Weight Yarn:
    Ecru - 36 ounces, (1,020 grams, 2,100 yards)
    Peach - 33 ounces, (940 grams, 1,925 yards)
Crochet hook, size G (4.00 mm) **or** size needed for gauge
Yarn needle

GAUGE: Rows 1-11 = 4"
           Each Strip = 3¹/4" wide

STRIP (Make 14)
CENTER
With Peach, ch 7 **loosely**.
Row 1 (Right side)**:** Dc in fourth ch from hook **(3 skipped chs count as first dc)**, ch 1, skip next ch, dc in last 2 chs: 4 dc.
Note: Loop a short piece of yarn around any stitch to mark Row 1 as **right** side and bottom edge.
Row 2: Ch 1, turn; sc in first 2 dc, sc in next ch-1 sp and in last 2 dc: 5 sc.
Row 3: Ch 3 **(counts as first dc, now and throughout)**, turn; dc in next sc, ch 1, skip next sc, dc in last 2 sc: 4 dc.
Rows 4-183: Repeat Rows 2 and 3, 90 times.
Finish off.

BORDER
Rnd 1: With **right** side facing, join Ecru with slip st in ch-1 sp on Row 183; ch 3, 4 dc in same sp; † working in end of rows, 3 dc in first row, (skip next row, 3 dc in next row) across †; working around beginning ch, 5 dc in next ch-1 sp, repeat from † to † once; join with slip st to first dc, finish off: 562 dc.
Rnd 2: With **right** side facing, join Peach with slip st in third dc to **right** of joining; ch 1, 2 sc in same st and in each of next 10 dc, sc in each dc across to last 3-dc group on same side, 2 sc in each of next 11 dc, sc in each dc across; join with slip st to first sc, finish off: 584 sc.

To work **Front Post treble crochet** *(abbreviated FPtr)*, YO twice, insert hook from **front** to **back** around post of st indicated, YO and pull up a loop, (YO and draw through 2 loops on hook) 3 times *(Fig. 12, page 118)*. Skip st behind FPtr.
Rnd 3: With **right** side facing and working in Back Loops Only *(Fig. 32, page 124)*, join Ecru with slip st in same st as joining; ch 1, sc in same st and in next 4 sc, work FPtr around second dc on Row 183, sc in next sc, (2 sc in next sc, sc in next sc) 4 times, work FPtr around third dc on Row 183, † sc in next 5 sc, working in **front** of previous rnds, tr in end of sc row on Center **below** next sc, (skip sc behind tr, sc in next 2 sc, working in **front** of previous rnds, tr in end of sc row on Center **below** next sc) 90 times, skip sc behind tr †, sc in next 5 sc, work FPtr around second dc on Row 1, sc in next sc, (2 sc in next sc, sc in next sc) 4 times, work FPtr around third dc on Row 1, repeat from † to † once; join with slip st to Back Loop Only of first sc, finish off: 592 sts.
Rnd 4: With **right** side facing and working in Back Loops Only, join Peach with slip st in first tr on either side; ch 1, sc in same st, † place marker around sc just made for joining placement, sc in next sc and in each st across to last tr on same side, sc in last tr, place marker around sc just made for joining placement †, sc in next sc and in each st around to first tr on opposite side, sc in next tr, repeat from † to † once, sc in each st around; join with slip st to first sc, finish off.

ASSEMBLY
Place two Strips with **wrong** sides together and bottom edges at the same end. Using Peach and working through inside loops only, whipstitch Strips together, beginning in first marked sc and ending in next marked sc *(Fig. 33a, page 125)*.

Join remaining Strips in same manner, always working in same direction.

FANCIFUL FLOWERS

Worked in brushed acrylic yarn, delicate violet blossoms with yellow French-knot centers accent this springtime throw. The afghan is a great carry-along project because the flowers are worked separately and then joined with cluster-stitch leaves and a graceful off-white border.

Finished Size: 47" x 63"

MATERIALS
Worsted Weight Brushed Acrylic Yarn:
Violet - 14 ounces, (400 grams, 890 yards)
Green - 11 ounces, (310 grams, 700 yards)
Off-White - 26 ounces, (740 grams, 1,650 yards)
Yellow - small amount
Crochet hook, size H (5.00 mm) **or** size needed for gauge

GAUGE: Each Flower = 3¼" (point to point)
Each Strip = 5¼" wide

FIRST STRIP
FLOWER (Make 20)
With Violet, ch 4; join with slip st to form a ring.
Rnd 1 (Right side): Ch 1, ★ sc in ring, ch 5, sc in second ch from hook and in next ch, hdc in next 2 chs; repeat from ★ 5 times **more**; join with slip st to first sc, finish off: 6 petals.
Note: Loop a short piece of yarn around any stitch to mark Rnd 1 as **right** side.

BORDER
To work **Cluster**, ★ YO twice, insert hook in st or sp indicated, YO and pull up a loop, (YO and draw through 2 loops on hook) twice; repeat from ★ 2 times **more**, YO and draw through all 4 loops on hook *(Figs. 17a & b, page 120)*.
Rnd 1: With **right** side facing, join Green with slip st in end of any petal; ch 1, sc in same sp, ch 4, sc in next petal, ch 2, work Cluster in sc **between** petals, ch 2, sc in next petal, † sc in any petal on **next** Flower, ★ (ch 2, work Cluster in sc **between** petals, ch 2, sc in next petal) twice, sc in any petal on **next** Flower; repeat from ★ 17 times **more**, ch 2, work Cluster in sc **between** petals, ch 2, sc in next petal, (ch 4, sc in next petal, ch 2, work Cluster in sc **between** petals, ch 2, sc in next petal) twice, sc in next free petal on **next** Flower, † (ch 2, work Cluster in sc **between** petals, ch 2, sc in next petal) twice, sc in next free petal on **next** Flower †, repeat from † to † 17 times **more**, ch 2, work Cluster in sc **between** petals, ch 2, sc in next petal, ch 4, sc in next petal, ch 2, work Cluster in sc **between** petals, ch 2; join with slip st to first sc, finish off.

Rnd 2: With **right** side facing, join Off-White with slip st in ch-4 sp to left of last joining; ch 3, YO twice, [insert hook in **same** sp, YO and pull up a loop, (YO and draw through 2 loops on hook) twice] 2 times, YO and draw through all 3 loops on hook, ch 3, work Cluster in same sp, ch 3, † sc in next sc, ch 3, ★ work Cluster in next ch-2 sp, (ch 1, work Cluster in next ch-2 sp) 3 times, ch 3, sc in next sc, ch 3; repeat from ★ 18 times **more**, (work Cluster, ch 3) twice in next ch-4 sp, work Cluster in next ch-2 sp, ch 3, work Cluster in next Cluster, ch 3, work Cluster in next ch-2 sp, ch 3 †, (work Cluster, ch 3) twice in next ch-4 sp, repeat from † to † once; join with slip st to top of first st: 166 Clusters.
Rnd 3: Ch 1, sc in same st, (sc, ch 3, sc) in next ch-3 sp, sc in next st and in next ch-3 sp, † ch 3, sc in next ch-3 sp and in next st, ★ (sc, ch 3, sc) in next ch-1 sp, sc in next ch-1 sp, (sc, ch 3, sc) in next ch-1 sp, sc in next st and in next ch-3 sp, ch 3, sc in next ch-3 sp and in next st; repeat from ★ 18 times **more**, (sc, ch 3, sc) in next ch-3 sp †, [sc in next st, (sc, ch 3, sc) in next ch-3 sp] 5 times, sc in next st and in next ch-3 sp, repeat from † to † once, [sc in next st, (sc, ch 3, sc) in next ch-3 sp] 4 times; join with slip st to first sc, finish off.

REMAINING 8 STRIPS
Work same as First Strip through Rnd 2.
Rnd 3 (Joining rnd): Ch 1, sc in same st, (sc, ch 3, sc) in next ch-3 sp, sc in next st and in next ch-3 sp, ch 3, sc in next ch-3 sp and in next st, † (sc, ch 3, sc) in next ch-1 sp, sc in next ch-1 sp, (sc, ch 3, sc) in next ch-1 sp, sc in next st and in next ch-3 sp, ch 3, sc in next ch-3 sp and in next st †, repeat from † to † 18 times **more**, (sc, ch 3, sc) in next ch-3 sp, [sc in next st, (sc, ch 3, sc) in next ch-3 sp] 5 times, sc in next st and in next ch-3 sp, ch 1, holding Strips with **wrong** sides together, slip st in corresponding ch-3 sp on **previous** Strip *(Fig. 28, page 122)*, ch 1, sc in next ch-3 sp on **new** Strip, ★ sc in next st and in next ch-1 sp, ch 1, slip st in next ch-3 sp on **previous** Strip, ch 1, sc in same sp on **new** Strip, sc in next 2 ch-1 sps, ch 1, slip st in next ch-3 sp on **previous** Strip, ch 1, sc in same sp on **new** Strip, sc in next st and in next ch-3 sp, ch 1, slip st in

next ch-3 sp on **previous Strip**, ch 1, sc in next ch-3 sp on **new Strip**; repeat from ★ 18 times **more**, [sc in next st, (sc, ch 3, sc) in next ch-3 sp] 5 times; join with slip st to first sc, finish off.

FINISHING

Using photo as a guide for placement, add Yellow French Knots to center of each Flower.

BABY-SOFT WRAPS

These comfy cover-ups will keep little ones nice and warm.
Using the same basic afghan pattern but different color combinations,
you can create totally different looks — and it's so easy!

SNOWY LULLABY
Finished Size: 32¹/2" x 45"

MATERIALS
Sport Weight Yarn:
21 ounces, (600 grams, 1,980 yards)
Crochet hook, size H (5.00 mm) **or** size needed for gauge
Yarn needle

GAUGE: Rows 1-4 = 2"
Each Strip = 3¹/4" wide

STRIP (Make 10)
CENTER
Row 1: Ch 4, (dc, tr, 2 dc) in fourth ch from hook: 5 sts.
Row 2 (Right side): Ch 2, turn; YO, insert hook in next dc, YO and pull up a loop, YO and draw through 2 loops on hook, YO, insert hook from **front** to **back** around post of next tr *(Fig. 9, page 118)*, YO and pull up a loop, YO and draw through 2 loops on hook, YO, insert hook in next dc, YO and pull up a loop, YO and draw through 2 loops on hook, YO, insert hook in top of beginning ch, YO and pull up a loop, YO and draw through 2 loops on hook, YO and draw through all 5 loops on hook: 1 st.
Note: Loop a short piece of yarn around stitch just made to mark bottom edge and to mark Row 2 as **right** side.
Row 3: Ch 4, do **not** turn; (dc, tr, 2 dc) in back ridge of fourth ch from hook *(Fig. 2c, page 116)*: 5 sts.
Row 4: Ch 2, turn; YO, insert hook in next dc, YO and pull up a loop, YO and draw through 2 loops on hook, YO, insert hook from **back** to **front** around post of next tr, YO and pull up a loop, YO and draw through 2 loops on hook, YO, insert hook in next dc, YO and pull up a loop, YO and draw through 2 loops on hook, YO, insert hook in top of beginning ch, YO and pull up a loop, YO and draw through 2 loops on hook, YO and draw through all 5 loops on hook: 1 st.
Row 5: Ch 4, do **not** turn; (dc, tr, 2 dc) in fourth ch from hook: 5 sts.
Rows 6-86: Repeat Rows 2-5, 20 times; then repeat Row 2 once **more**.
Do **not** finish off.

BORDER
To work **Picot**, ch 3, 2 dc in third ch from hook
Rnd 1: Working in end of rows, (slip st, ch 1, sc) in same row, † ch 2, sc in next row, work Picot, sc in next row, ★ ch 1, sc in next row, work Picot, sc in next row; repeat from ★ across to last row, ch 2, sc in last row, work Picot †, sc in opposite end of same row, repeat from † to † once; join with slip st to first sc.
Rnd 2: Slip st in first ch-2 sp, ch 3 **(counts as first dc, now and throughout)**, dc in same sp, † ch 2, sc in top ch of next Picot, ★ ch 1, 2 dc in next ch-1 sp, ch 1, sc in top ch of next Picot; repeat from ★ across to next ch-2 sp, ch 2, (2 dc, ch 2) twice in next ch-2 sp, sc in top ch of next Picot †, (ch 2, 2 dc) twice in next ch-2 sp, repeat from † to † once, ch 2, 2 dc in same sp as beginning ch-3, ch 2; join with slip st to first dc.
Rnd 3: Slip st in next dc and in first ch-2 sp, ch 3, 2 dc in same sp and in next ch-1 sp, (3 dc in next sp, 2 dc in next sp) across to corner ch-2 sp, † (3 dc, ch 2, 3 dc) in corner ch-2 sp, 2 dc in each of next 2 ch-2 sps, (3 dc, ch 2, 3 dc) in next corner ch-2 sp †, (2 dc in next sp, 3 dc in next sp) across to next corner ch-2 sp, repeat from † to † once; join with slip st to first dc, finish off.

ASSEMBLY
Place two Strips with **wrong** sides together and bottom edges at the same end. Working through inside loops only, whipstitch Strips together, beginning in second ch of first corner ch-2 and ending in first ch of next corner ch-2 *(Fig. 33a, page 125)*.

Join remaining Strips in same manner, always working in same direction.

BLUE & WHITE BLISS
Finished Size: 32¹/2" x 45"

MATERIALS
Sport Weight Yarn:
Blue - 16 ounces, (450 grams, 1,485 yards)
White - 5¹/4 ounces, (150 grams, 500 yards)
Crochet hook, size H (5.00 mm) **or** size needed for gauge
Yarn needle

GAUGE: Rows 1-4 = 2"
Each Strip = 3¹/4" wide

STRIP (Make 10)
CENTER

Row 1: With Blue ch 4, (dc, tr, 2 dc) in fourth ch from hook: 5 sts.

Row 2 (Right side)**:** Ch 2, turn; YO, insert hook in next dc, YO and pull up a loop, YO and draw through 2 loops on hook, YO, insert hook from **front** to **back** around post of next tr *(Fig. 9, page 118)*, YO and pull up a loop, YO and draw through 2 loops on hook, YO, insert hook in next dc, YO and pull up a loop, YO and draw through 2 loops on hook, YO, insert hook in top of beginning ch, YO and pull up a loop, YO and draw through 2 loops on hook, YO and draw through all 5 loops on hook: 1 st.

Note: Loop a short piece of yarn around stitch just made to mark bottom edge and to mark Row 2 as **right** side.

Row 3: Ch 4, do **not** turn; (dc, tr, 2 dc) in back ridge of fourth ch from hook *(Fig. 2c, page 116)*: 5 sts.

Row 4: Ch 2, turn; YO, insert hook in next dc, YO and pull up a loop, YO and draw through 2 loops on hook, YO, insert hook from **back** to **front** around post of next tr, YO and pull up a loop, YO and draw through 2 loops on hook, YO, insert hook in next dc, YO and pull up a loop, YO and draw through 2 loops on hook, YO, insert hook in top of beginning ch, YO and pull up a loop, YO and draw through 2 loops on hook, YO and draw through all 5 loops on hook: 1 st.

Row 5: Ch 4, do **not** turn; (dc, tr, 2 dc) in fourth ch from hook: 5 sts.

Rows 6-86: Repeat Rows 2-5, 20 times; then repeat Row 2 once **more**.

Finish off.

BORDER

To work **Picot**, ch 3, 2 dc in third ch from hook.

Rnd 1: With **right** side facing and working in end of rows, join White with slip st around beginning ch-2 on last row; ch 1, sc in same row, † work Picot, sc in opposite side of same row, ch 2, sc in next row, work Picot, sc in next row, ★ ch 1, sc in next row, work Picot, sc in next row; repeat from ★ across to last row, ch 2 †, sc in last row, repeat from † to † once; join with slip st to first sc, finish off.

Rnd 2: With **right** side facing, join Blue with slip st in first ch-2 sp; ch 3 (**counts as first dc, now and throughout**), dc in same sp, † ch 2, sc in top ch of next Picot, ★ ch 1, 2 dc in next ch-1 sp, ch 1, sc in top ch of next Picot; repeat from ★ across to next ch-2 sp, ch 2, (2 dc, ch 2) twice in next ch-2 sp, sc in top ch of next Picot †, (ch 2, 2 dc) twice in next ch-2 sp, repeat from † to † once, ch 2, 2 dc in same sp as beginning ch-3, ch 2; join with slip st to first dc.

Rnd 3: Slip st in next dc and in first ch-2 sp, ch 3, 2 dc in same sp and in next ch-1 sp, (3 dc in next sp, 2 dc in next sp) across to corner ch-2 sp, † (3 dc, ch 2, 3 dc) in corner ch-2 sp, 2 dc in each of next 2 ch-2 sps, (3 dc, ch 2, 3 dc) in next corner ch-2 sp †, (2 dc in next sp, 3 dc in next sp) across to corner ch-2 sp; repeat from † to † once; join with slip st to first dc, finish off.

ASSEMBLY

Place two Strips with **wrong** sides together and bottom edge at the same end. Using Blue and working through inside loops only, whipstitch Strips together, beginning in second ch of first corner ch-2 and ending in first ch of next corner ch-2 (**Fig. 33a, page 125**).

Join remaining Strips in same manner, always working in same direction.

CINNAMON STICKS

Worked in easy strips of double crochets and chain spaces, our cinnamony red afghan is great for beginners! Lush tassels enhance the ends of this homey hearthside comforter.

Finished Size: 47" x 63"

MATERIALS

Worsted Weight Yarn:
51 ounces, (1,450 grams, 3,500 yards)
Crochet hook, size G (4.00 mm) **or** size needed for gauge
Yarn needle

GAUGE: In pattern, 5 sps and 9 rows = 3³/4"
Each Strip = 5¹/4" wide

STRIP (Make 9)

Ch 5 **loosely**.

Row 1 (Right side): Dc in fourth ch from hook and in last ch: 3 sts.

Note: Loop a short piece of yarn around any stitch to mark Row 1 as **right** side and bottom edge.

Row 2: Ch 3 (**counts as first dc, now and throughout**), turn; 2 dc in same st, ch 1, skip next dc, 3 dc in top of beginning ch: 6 dc.

Row 3: Ch 3, turn; 2 dc in same st, ch 1, 3 dc in next ch-1 sp, ch 1, skip next 2 dc, 3 dc in last dc: 9 dc.

Rows 4-6: Ch 3, turn; 2 dc in same st, ch 1, (3 dc in next ch-1 sp, ch 1) across to last 3 dc, skip next 2 dc, 3 dc in last dc: 18 dc.

Row 7: Ch 4 (**counts as first dc plus ch 1**), turn; (3 dc in next ch-1 sp, ch 1) across to last 3 dc, skip next 2 dc, dc in last dc: 17 dc.

Row 8: Ch 3, turn; 2 dc in next ch-1 sp, (ch 1, 3 dc in next ch-1 sp) across: 18 dc.

Rows 9-146: Repeat Rows 7 and 8, 69 times.

Rows 147-149: Ch 3, turn; 2 dc in next ch-1 sp, ch 1, (3 dc in next ch-1 sp, ch 1) across to last ch-1 sp, 2 dc in last ch-1 sp, skip next 2 dc, dc in last dc: 9 dc.

Row 150: Ch 3, turn; 2 dc in next ch-1 sp, ch 1, 2 dc in next ch-1 sp, skip next 2 dc, dc in last dc: 6 dc.

Row 151: Ch 3, turn; 2 dc in next ch-1 sp, skip next 2 dc, dc in last dc: 4 dc.

Edging: Ch 1, do **not** turn; † working in end of rows, 2 sc in each of first 6 rows, place marker around last sc made for joining placement, 2 sc in each of next 139 rows, sc in next row, place marker around sc just made for joining placement, sc in same row, 2 sc in each of last 5 rows †; working in free loops of beginning ch *(Fig. 31b, page 124)*, skip first ch, 3 sc in next ch (at base of center dc), skip next ch, repeat from † to † once; working across Row 151, skip first 2 dc, 3 sc in next dc, skip last dc; join with slip st to first sc, finish off.

ASSEMBLY

Place two Strips with **wrong** sides together and bottom edges at the same end. Working through both loops, whipstitch Strips together, beginning in first marked sc and ending in next marked sc *(Fig. 33b, page 125)*.

Join remaining Strips in same manner, always working in same direction.

TASSELS

Make 18 tassels *(Figs. 35a & b, page 126)*.
Attach one tassel to each end of each Strip.

RUFFLED TREASURE

This feminine throw features ruffles of ecru shell stitches. The center strips on our vintage treasure are fashioned from rose-colored shells.

Finished Size: 52¹/₂ " x 72"

MATERIALS
Worsted Weight Yarn:
Rose - 48¹/₂ ounces, (1,380 grams, 3,185 yards)
Ecru - 19 ounces, (540 grams, 1,250 yards)
Crochet hook, size G (4.00 mm) **or** size needed for gauge
Yarn needle

GAUGE: 16 dc = 4"
Rows 1-6 = 4"
Each Strip = 3¹/₂" wide

STRIP (Make 15)
CENTER
To work **Shell**, (3 dc, ch 2, 3 dc) in st or sp indicated.
With Rose, ch 11 **loosely**.
Row 1 (Right side)**:** Dc in fourth ch from hook, place marker around last dc made for Ruffle placement, skip next 2 chs, work Shell in next ch, skip next 2 chs, dc in last 2 chs: 10 sts.
Note: Loop a short piece of yarn around any stitch to mark Row 1 as **right** side and bottom edge.
Rows 2-106: Ch 3 (**counts as first dc, now and throughout**), turn; dc in next dc, work Shell in next ch-2 sp, skip next 3 dc, dc in last 2 sts.
Row 107: Ch 3, turn; dc in next dc, ch 2, sc in next ch-2 sp, ch 2, skip next 3 dc, dc in last 2 dc; finish off: 2 ch-2 sps.

RUFFLE
With **right** side facing and working in **front** of first dc and around second dc on each row across (between first dc and Shell), join Ecru with slip st around marked dc; ch 3, 4 dc around same dc, (sc around next dc, 5 dc around next dc) across; working across Row 107, sc in first ch-2 sp, 5 dc in next sc, sc in last ch-2 sp; working in **front** of first dc and around second dc on each row across (between Shell and last dc), 5 dc around first dc (on Row 107), (sc around next dc, 5 dc around next dc) across; working around beginning ch, sc in first ch-2 sp, 5 dc in free loop of ch at base of Shell *(Fig. 31b, page 124)*, sc in last ch-2 sp; join with slip st to first dc, finish off.

TRIM
FIRST SIDE
With **right** side of long edge facing and working **behind** Ruffle and in end of rows on Center, join Rose with slip st in first row; ch 3, dc in same row, 2 dc in next row, (3 dc in each of next 2 rows, 2 dc in next row) across; finish off: 284 dc.

SECOND SIDE
Work same as First Side.

ASSEMBLY
Place two Strips with **wrong** sides together and bottom edges at the same end. Using Rose and working through inside loops only, whipstitch Strips together, beginning in first dc of Trim and ending in last dc of Trim *(Fig. 33a, page 125)*.

Join remaining Strips in same manner, always working in same direction.

CUDDLY CLUSTERS

Made from sport weight yarn, our cuddly cover-up is a blanket of white and yellow clusters enhanced with light green chain stitches and half double crochets. It'll make a heartwarming afghan for a newborn!

Finished Size: 36" x 44"

MATERIALS
Sport Weight Yarn:
White - 7¹/4 ounces, (210 grams, 725 yards)
Yellow - 3¹/4 ounces, (90 grams, 325 yards)
Green - 2 ounces, (60 grams, 200 yards)
Crochet hook, size H (5.00 mm) **or** size needed for gauge

GAUGE: (ch 2, Cluster) 5 times = 3"
Each Strip = 4" wide

FIRST STRIP
To work **Cluster,** ★ YO, insert hook in st or sp indicated, YO and pull up a loop, YO and draw through 2 loops on hook; repeat from ★ 2 times **more,** YO and draw through all 4 loops on hook *(Figs. 17a & b, page 120).*
With White, ch 195 **loosely.**
Rnd 1 (Right side): YO, insert hook in third ch from hook, YO and pull up a loop, YO and draw through 2 loops on hook, YO insert hook in **same** ch, YO and pull up a loop, YO and draw through 2 loops on hook, YO and draw through all 3 loops on hook **(beginning Cluster made),** (ch 3, work Cluster in same ch) twice, (ch 2, skip next 2 chs, work Cluster in next ch) across, (ch 3, work Cluster in same ch) twice; working in free loops of beginning ch *(Fig. 31b, page 124),* (ch 2, skip next 2 chs, work Cluster in next ch) across to last 2 chs, ch 2, skip last 2 chs; join with slip st to top of beginning Cluster, finish off: 132 Clusters.
Note: Loop a short piece of yarn around any stitch to mark Rnd 1 as **right** side.
Rnd 2: With **right** side facing, join Green with slip st in same st as joining; ch 4 **(counts as first hdc plus ch 2, now and throughout),** hdc in same st, † ch 3, (hdc, ch 3) 3 times in next Cluster, (hdc, ch 2) twice in next Cluster, hdc in next Cluster, (ch 2, hdc in next Cluster) 62 times †, (ch 2, hdc) twice in next Cluster, repeat from † to † once, ch 2; join with slip st to first hdc, finish off.

Rnd 3: With **right** side facing, skip first ch-2 sp and join White with slip st in next ch-3 sp; ch 4, † skip next hdc, work Cluster in next ch, ch 2, hdc in same ch-3 sp, ch 2, skip next hdc, work (Cluster, ch 3, Cluster) in next ch, ch 2, hdc in same ch-3 sp, ch 2, skip next hdc, work Cluster in next ch, ch 2, hdc in same ch-3 sp, ch 2, (skip next hdc, work Cluster in next ch, ch 2) 67 times †, hdc in same ch-3 sp, ch 2, repeat from † to † once; join with slip st to second ch of beginning ch-4, finish off: 142 Clusters.
Rnd 4: With **right** side facing, join Yellow with slip st in first Cluster to left of last joining; ch 1, (sc, ch 3, sc) in same st, ch 1, skip next hdc, work Cluster in next ch, ch 1, (sc, ch 3, sc) in next Cluster, ch 1, † work (Cluster, ch 3, Cluster) in next ch-3 sp, ch 1, [(sc, ch 3, sc) in next Cluster, ch 1, skip next hdc, work Cluster in next ch, ch 1] twice, (sc, ch 3, sc) in next Cluster, ch 1, [work Cluster in next Cluster, ch 1, (sc, ch 3, sc) in next Cluster, ch 1] 33 times †, [skip next hdc, work Cluster in next ch, ch 1, (sc, ch 3, sc) in next Cluster, ch 1] twice, repeat from † to † once, skip next hdc, work Cluster in next ch, ch 1; join with slip st to first sc, finish off.

REMAINING 8 STRIPS
Work same as First Strip through Rnd 3.
Rnd 4 (Joining rnd): With **right** side facing, join Yellow with slip st in first Cluster to left of last joining; ch 1, (sc, ch 3, sc) in same st, ch 1, skip next hdc, work Cluster in next ch, ch 1, (sc, ch 3, sc) in next Cluster, ch 1, † work (Cluster, ch 3, Cluster) in next ch-3 sp, ch 1, [(sc, ch 3, sc) in next Cluster, ch 1, skip next hdc, work Cluster in next ch, ch 1] twice †, (sc, ch 3, sc) in next Cluster, ch 1, [work Cluster in next Cluster, ch 1, (sc, ch 3, sc) in next Cluster, ch 1] 33 times, [skip next hdc, work Cluster in next ch, ch 1, (sc, ch 3, sc) in next Cluster, ch 1] twice, repeat from † to † once, sc in next Cluster, ch 1, holding Strips with **wrong** sides together, slip st in corresponding ch-3 sp on **previous Strip** *(Fig. 28, page 122),* ch 1, sc in same Cluster on **new Strip,** ch 1, ★ work Cluster in next Cluster, ch 1, sc in next Cluster, ch 1, slip st in next ch-3 sp on **previous Strip,** ch 1, sc in same Cluster on **new Strip,** ch 1; repeat from ★ across, skip next hdc, work Cluster in next ch, ch 1; join with slip st to first sc, finish off.

TRULY VICTORIAN

*Worked entirely in plush green brushed acrylic yarn, this
Victorian-style afghan is delicately detailed with double crochets, trebles,
and chain spaces. Scalloped ends complement the nostalgic look.*

Finished Size: 48" x 63"

MATERIALS

Worsted Weight Brushed Acrylic Yarn:
   44 ounces, (1,250 grams, 2,790 yards)
Crochet hook, size J (6.00 mm) **or** size needed for gauge

GAUGE: Center = 3¾" wide and 6 rows = 5"
   Each Strip = 6" wide

FIRST STRIP
CENTER
Ch 12 **loosely**.
Row 1 (Right side): Dc in fourth ch from hook **(3 skipped chs count as first dc)**, skip next 2 chs, 3 dc in each of next 2 chs, skip next 2 chs, dc in last 2 chs.
Note: Loop a short piece of yarn around any stitch to mark Row 1 as **right** side and bottom edge.
Rows 2-77: Ch 3 **(counts as first dc, now and throughout)**, turn; dc in next dc, skip next dc, 3 dc in next dc, skip next 2 dc, 3 dc in next dc, skip next dc, dc in last 2 dc.
Do **not** finish off.

BORDER
Rnd 1: Ch 3, working in end of rows, 4 dc in first row, (sc in next row, 5 dc in next row) across; working around beginning ch, skip first 2 dc, sc in next ch-2 sp, skip next 3 dc, 7 tr in sp **before** next dc **(Fig. 27, page 122)**, sc in next ch-2 sp; working in end of rows, 5 dc in first row, (sc in next row, 5 dc in next row) across; working across last row, skip first 2 dc, sc in sp **before** next dc, skip next 3 dc, 7 tr in sp **before** next dc, skip next 3 dc, sc in sp **before** next dc; join with slip st to first dc: 78 5-dc groups.

Rnd 2: Slip st in next 2 dc, ch 1, sc in same st, skip next 2 dc, 5 dc in next sc, ★ (skip next 2 dc, sc in next dc, skip next 2 dc, 5 dc in next sc) across to next 7-tr group, sc in next tr, skip next 2 tr, 9 tr in next tr, skip next 2 tr, sc in next tr, 5 dc in next sc; repeat from ★ once **more**; join with slip st to first sc, finish off.

REMAINING 7 STRIPS
Work same as First Strip through Rnd 1 of Border.
Rnd 2 (Joining rnd): Slip st in next 2 dc, ch 1, sc in same st, skip next 2 dc, 5 dc in next sc, (skip next 2 dc, sc in next dc, skip next 2 dc, 5 dc in next sc) across to next 7-tr group, sc in next tr, skip next 2 tr, 9 tr in next tr, skip next 2 tr, sc in next tr, 5 dc in next sc, skip next 2 dc, sc in next dc, skip next 2 dc, 3 dc in next sc, holding Strips with **wrong** sides together and bottom edges at the same end, slip st in center dc of corresponding 5-dc group on **previous Strip (Fig. 28, page 122)**, slip st in last dc made on **new** Strip, 2 dc in same st as last 3 dc made, skip next 2 dc, sc in next dc, ★ skip next 2 dc, 3 dc in next sc, slip st in center dc of next 5-dc group on **previous Strip**, slip st in last dc made on **new Strip**, 2 dc in same st as last 3 dc made, skip next 2 dc, sc in next dc; repeat from ★ 36 times **more**, skip next 2 dc, 5 dc in next sc, sc in next tr, skip next 2 tr, 9 tr in next tr, skip next 2 tr, sc in next tr, 5 dc in next sc; join with slip st to first sc, finish off.

FORMAL GARDEN

This floral-hued afghan is a blanket of dramatic zigzags. A handy placement diagram makes assembling the uniquely shaped wrap a snap.

Finished Size: 54" x 71"

MATERIALS

Worsted Weight Yarn:
Off-White - 23 ounces, (650 grams, 1,460 yards)
Green - 10 ounces, (280 grams, 635 yards)
Lt Green - 7 ounces, (200 grams, 445 yards)
Purple - 10 ounces, (280 grams, 635 yards)
Lavender - 10 ounces, (280 grams, 635 yards)
Crochet hook, size I (5.50 mm) **or** size needed for gauge
Yarn needle

GAUGE: 12 sc and 14 rows = 4"
Each Strip = 6" wide

STRIP (Make 9)

With Off-White, ch 206 **loosely**.

Rnd 1: Sc in second ch from hook, place marker around last sc made for Rnd 2 joining, skip next 2 chs, 5 dc in next ch, (skip next 2 chs, sc in next ch, skip next 2 chs, 5 dc in next ch) across to last 3 chs, skip next 2 chs, 5 sc in last ch; working in free loops of beginning ch *(Fig. 31b, page 124)*, skip next 2 chs, 5 dc in next ch, (skip next 2 chs, sc in next ch, skip next 2 chs, 5 dc in next ch) 33 times, skip next 2 chs, 4 sc in same ch as first sc; join with slip st to first sc, finish off: 68 5-dc groups.

Note: Loop a short piece of yarn around the **back** of any stitch on Rnd 1 to mark **right** side.

Rnd 2: With **right** side facing, join Green with sc in marked sc *(see Joining With Sc, page 124)*; hdc in next sc, (dc, tr, dc) in next sc, place marker around last tr made for Rnd 3 joining, hdc in next sc, (sc in next sc, hdc in next dc, dc in next dc, tr in next dc, dc in next dc, hdc in next dc) across to next 5-sc group, sc in next sc, hdc in next sc, (dc, tr, dc) in next sc, place marker around last tr made, hdc in next sc, (sc in next sc, hdc in next dc, dc in next dc, tr in next dc, dc in next dc, hdc in next dc) across; join with slip st to first sc, finish off: 420 sts.

To **decrease**, pull up a loop in next 3 sts, YO and draw through all 4 loops on hook (**counts as one sc**).

Rnd 3: With **wrong** side facing, join Lt Green with sc in first marked tr on Rnd 2; 2 sc in same st, place marker around center sc of 3-sc group just made for Rnd 4 joining, sc in next 5 sts, 3 sc in next tr, (sc in next dc, decrease, sc in next dc, 3 sc in next tr) to within 5 sts of next marked tr, sc in next 5 sts, 3 sc in next tr, place marker around center sc of 3-sc group just made, sc in next 5 sts, 3 sc in next tr, (sc in next dc, decrease, sc in next dc, 3 sc in next tr) across to last 5 sts, sc in last 5 sts; join with slip st to first sc, finish off: 428 sc.

Rnd 4: With **right** side facing, join Purple with sc in either marked sc on Rnd 3; 4 sc in same st, place marker around center sc of 5-sc group just made for Rnd 5 joining, sc in next 7 sc, 5 sc in next sc, (sc in next sc, decrease, sc in next sc, 5 sc in next sc) across to within 7 sc of next marked sc, sc in next 7 sc, 5 sc in next sc, place marker around center sc of 5-sc group just made, sc in next 7 sc, 5 sc in next sc, (sc in next sc, decrease, sc in next sc, 5 sc in next sc) across to last 7 sc, sc in last 7 sc; join with slip st to first sc, finish off: 576 sc.

Rnd 5: With **wrong** side facing, join Lavender with sc in either marked sc on Rnd 4; 2 sc in same st, place marker around center sc of 3-sc group just made for Rnd 6 joining, sc in next 11 sc, 3 sc in next sc, (sc in next 2 sc, decrease, sc in next 2 sc, 3 sc in next sc) across to within 11 sc of next marked sc, sc in next 11 sc, 3 sc in next sc, place marker around center sc of 3-sc group just made, sc in next 11 sc, 3 sc in next sc, (sc in next 2 sc, decrease, sc in next 2 sc, 3 sc in next sc) across to last 11 sc, sc in last 11 sc; join with slip st to first sc, finish off: 584 sc.

Rnd 6: With **right** side facing, join Off-White with sc in either marked sc on Rnd 5; 4 sc in same st, sc in next 13 sc, 5 sc in next sc, place marker around center sc of 5-sc group just made for joining placement, (sc in next 2 sc, decrease, sc in next 2 sc, 5 sc in next sc) across to within 13 sc of next marked sc, sc in next 3 sc, place marker around last sc made for joining placement, sc in next 10 sc, 5 sc in next sc, sc in next 11 sc, place marker around last sc made for joining placement, sc in next 2 sc, 5 sc in next sc, (sc in next 2 sc, decrease, sc in next 2 sc, 5 sc in next sc) across to last 13 sc, place marker around center sc of 5-sc group just made for joining placement, sc in last 13 sc; join with slip st to first sc, finish off.

ASSEMBLY

Place Strips together, matching marked stitches as shown in Placement Diagram.

With **wrong** sides together, using Off-White and working through inside loops only, whipstitch Strips together, beginning in first marked stitch and ending in next marked stitch (**Fig. 33a, page 125**).

Join remaining Strips in same manner, always working in same direction.

COUNTRY FAIR FAVORITES

Like old-fashioned favorites found at a country fair, this plush pair has blue-ribbon appeal! One afghan, resembling a blanket of summertime peaches, is fashioned from shells worked back-to-back. Finished with fringe, the other wrap features a shell-stitch latticework in ecru, peach, and green.

PEACH ORCHARD

Finished Size: 47" x 63"

MATERIALS
Worsted Weight Yarn:
  Peach - 30$\frac{1}{2}$ ounces, (870 grams, 1,780 yards)
  Ecru - 21$\frac{1}{2}$ ounces, (610 grams, 1,255 yards)
Crochet hook, size I (5.50 mm) **or** size needed
  for gauge

GAUGE: 5 Shells = 9"
  Each Strip = 4$\frac{1}{4}$" wide

FIRST STRIP

To work **Shell**, (3 dc, ch 2, 3 dc) in st indicated.

With Peach, ch 206 **loosely**.

Rnd 1 (Right side): Sc in second ch from hook, ch 1, skip next 2 chs, work Shell in next ch, ch 1, † skip next 2 chs, sc in next ch, ch 1, skip next 2 chs, work Shell in next ch, ch 1 †, repeat from † to † across to last 3 chs, skip next 2 chs, 3 sc in last ch; working in free loops of beginning ch **(Fig. 31b, page 124)**, ch 1, skip next 2 chs, work Shell in next ch, ch 1, repeat from † to † 33 times, skip next 2 chs, 2 sc in same ch as first sc; join with slip st to first sc, finish off: 68 Shells.

Note: Loop a short piece of yarn around any stitch to mark Rnd 1 as **right** side.

Rnd 2: With **right** side facing, join Ecru with slip st in last sc made; † ch 6, sc in next Shell (ch-2 sp), ★ ch 3, working **around** sc, tr in same ch as next sc on Center, ch 3, sc in next Shell; repeat from ★ across, ch 6, skip next sc †, slip st in next sc, repeat from † to † once; join with slip st to first slip st: 132 ch-3 sps.

Rnd 3: Slip st in first sp, ch 3 **(counts as first dc, now and throughout)**, work (2 dc, ch 1, 3 dc, ch 2, 3 dc) in same sp, † ch 1, (3 dc in next ch-3 sp, ch 1) across to next ch-6 sp, work (3 dc, ch 2, 3 dc, ch 1, 3 dc) in ch-6 sp, ch 1 †, work (3 dc, ch 1, 3 dc, ch 2, 3 dc) in next ch-6 sp, repeat from † to † once; join with slip st to first dc, finish off.

Rnd 4: With **right** side facing, join Peach with slip st in any corner ch-2 sp; ch 3, (2 dc, ch 2, 3 dc) in same sp, ch 1, (3 dc in next ch-1 sp, ch 1) across to next corner ch-2 sp, ★ (3 dc, ch 2, 3 dc) in next ch-2 sp, ch 1, (3 dc in next ch-1 sp, ch 1) across to next corner ch-2 sp; repeat from ★ around; join with slip st to first dc, finish off.

REMAINING 10 STRIPS

Work same as First Strip through Rnd 3.

Rnd 4 (Joining rnd): With **right** side facing and holding Strip vertically, join Peach with slip st in top left corner ch-2 sp; ch 3, (2 dc, ch 2, 3 dc) in same sp, ch 1, (3 dc in next ch-1 sp, ch 1) across to next corner ch-2 sp, (3 dc, ch 2, 3 dc) in ch-2 sp, ch 1, (3 dc in next ch-1 sp, ch 1) across to next corner ch-2 sp, 3 dc in ch-2 sp, ch 1, holding Strips with **wrong** sides together, slip st in corner ch-2 sp on **previous** Strip **(Fig. 28, page 122)**, ch 1, 3 dc in same ch-2 sp on **new** Strip, ch 1, slip st in next ch-1 sp on **previous** Strip, ★ 3 dc in next ch-1 sp on **new** Strip, ch 1, slip st in next ch-1 sp on **previous** Strip; repeat from ★ across to next corner ch-2 sp on **new** Strip, 3 dc in ch-2 sp, ch 1, slip st in next corner ch-2 sp on **previous** Strip, ch 1, 3 dc in same ch-2 sp on **new** Strip, ch 1, (3 dc in next ch-1 sp, ch 1) across; join with slip st to first dc, finish off.

FRINGED FANCY

Finished Size: 45" x 64"

MATERIALS

Worsted Weight Yarn:
Ecru - 25 ounces, (710 grams, 1,460 yards)
Peach - 9 ounces, (260 grams, 525 yards)
Green - 10 ounces, (280 grams, 585 yards)
Crochet hook, size H (5.00 mm) **or** size needed for gauge

GAUGE: Each Strip = 3½" wide and 10 rows = 8"

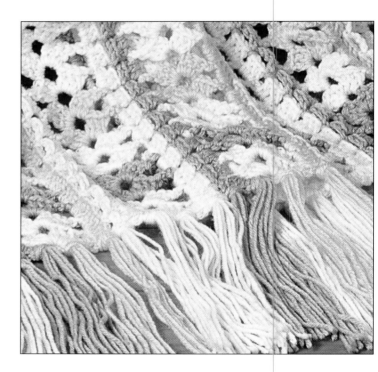

FIRST STRIP
CENTER

With Ecru, ch 4; join with slip st to form a ring.

Row 1 (Right side): Ch 4, (3 dc, ch 3, 3 dc, ch 1, dc) in ring.

Note: Loop a short piece of yarn around any stitch to mark Row 1 as **right** side and bottom edge.

Row 2: Ch 4 **(counts as first dc plus ch 1, now and throughout)**, turn; (3 dc, ch 3, 3 dc) in next ch-3 sp, ch 1, skip next ch, dc in next ch changing to Green **(Fig. 30a, page 124)**.

Row 3: Ch 4, turn; (3 dc, ch 3, 3 dc) in next ch-3 sp, ch 1, skip next 3 dc, dc in last dc.

Row 4: Ch 4, turn; (3 dc, ch 3, 3 dc) in next ch-3 sp, ch 1, skip next 3 dc, dc in last dc changing to Ecru.

Row 5: Ch 4, turn; (3 dc, ch 3, 3 dc) in next ch-3 sp, ch 1, skip next 3 dc, dc in last dc.

Row 6: Ch 4, turn; (3 dc, ch 3, 3 dc) in next ch-3 sp, ch 1, skip next 3 dc, dc in last dc changing to Peach.

Row 7: Ch 4, turn; (3 dc, ch 3, 3 dc) in next ch-3 sp, ch 1, skip next 3 dc, dc in last dc.

Row 8: Ch 4, turn; (3 dc, ch 3, 3 dc) in next ch-3 sp, ch 1, skip next 3 dc, dc in last dc changing to Ecru.

Rows 9-11: Ch 4, turn; (3 dc, ch 3, 3 dc) in next ch-3 sp, ch 1, skip next 3 dc, dc in last dc.

Row 12: Ch 4, turn; (3 dc, ch 3, 3 dc) in next ch-3 sp, ch 1, skip next 3 dc, dc in last dc changing to Green.

Rows 13-80: Repeat Rows 3-12, 6 times; then repeat Rows 3-10 once **more**.
Finish off.

BORDER

With **right** side facing, join Ecru with slip st in beginning ring, ch 1; † working in end of rows, (3 dc, ch 2, 3 dc) in first row, ch 1, (3 dc in next row, ch 1) across to last row, (3 dc, ch 2, 3 dc) in last row, ch 1 †, slip st in next ch-3 sp, ch 1, repeat from † to † once; join with slip st to first slip st, finish off.

SECOND STRIP
CENTER
Work same as First Strip.

JOINING

With **right** side facing, join Peach with slip st in beginning ring, ch 1; working in end of rows, (3 dc, ch 2, 3 dc) in first row, ch 1, (3 dc in next row, ch 1) across to last row, (3 dc, ch 2, 3 dc) in last row, ch 1, slip st in next ch-3 sp changing to Green *(Fig. 30b, page 124)*, ch 1; working in end of rows, 3 dc in first row, ch 1, holding Strips with **wrong** sides together and bottom edges at same end, slip st in corner ch-2 sp on **previous Strip** *(Fig. 28, page 122)*, ch 1, 3 dc in same row on **new Strip**, ch 1, slip st in next ch-1 sp on **previous Strip**, ★ 3 dc in next row on **new Strip**, ch 1, slip st in next ch-1 sp on **previous Strip**; repeat from ★ across to last row on **new Strip**, 3 dc in last row on **new Strip**, ch 1, slip st in next ch-2 sp on **previous Strip**, ch 1, 3 dc in same row on **new Strip**, ch 1; join with slip st to first slip st, finish off.

THIRD STRIP
CENTER
Work same as First Strip.

JOINING

With **right** side facing, join Ecru with slip st in beginning ring, ch 1; working in end of rows, (3 dc, ch 2, 3 dc) in first row, ch 1, (3 dc in next row, ch 1) across to last row, (3 dc, ch 2, 3 dc) in last row, ch 1, slip st in next ch-3 sp, ch 1; working in end of rows, 3 dc in first row, ch 1, holding Strips with **wrong** sides together and bottom edges at same end, slip st in corner ch-2 sp on **previous Strip**, ch 1, 3 dc in same row on **new Strip**, ch 1, slip st in next ch-1 sp on **previous Strip**, ★ 3 dc in next row on **new Strip**, ch 1, slip st in next ch-1 sp on **previous Strip**; repeat from ★ across to last row on **new Strip**, 3 dc in last row on **new Strip**, ch 1, slip st in next ch-2 sp on **previous Strip**, ch 1, 3 dc in same row on **new Strip**, ch 1; join with slip st to first slip st, finish off.

REMAINING 10 STRIPS

Repeat Second and Third Strips, 5 times.

Holding 4 strands of corresponding color together, add fringe evenly across short edges of afghan *(Figs. 34a & b, page 126)*.

EASYGOING AFGHAN

*Stitched in soothing shades of blue, this easygoing afghan offers
lazy-day comfort. The simple wrap is fashioned using double crochets
and front post double crochets, so it works up in no time.*

Finished Size: 46" x 63"

MATERIALS
Worsted Weight Yarn:
Blue - 35 ounces, (990 grams, 1,980) yards
Lt Blue - 8 ounces, (230 grams, 450 yards
Crochet hooks, sizes I (5.50 mm) **and** J (6.00 mm) **or**
sizes needed for gauge
Yarn needle

GAUGE: With larger size hook,
Center = 3³/4" wide and 5 rows = 3"
Each Strip = 5³/4" wide

STRIP (Make 8)
CENTER
With larger hook and Blue, ch 17 **loosely**.
Row 1 (Right side): Dc in fourth ch from hook **(3 skipped
chs count as first dc)**, skip next 2 chs, 5 dc in next ch,
skip next 2 chs, dc in next ch, skip next 2 chs, 5 dc in next
ch, skip next 2 chs, dc in last 2 chs: 15 dc.
Note: Loop a short piece of yarn around any stitch to mark
Row 1 as **right** side and bottom edge.
To work **Front Post double crochet (abbreviated FPdc)**,
YO, insert hook from **front** to **back** around post of st
indicated, YO and pull up a loop **(Fig. 11, page 118)**,
(YO and draw through 2 loops on hook) twice .
Row 2: Ch 3 **(counts as first dc, now and throughout)**,
work FPdc around next dc, ★ skip next 2 dc, 5 dc in next
dc, skip next 2 dc, work FPdc around next dc; repeat from
★ once **more**, dc in last dc.
Rows 3-99: Ch 3, turn; work FPdc around next FPdc,
★ skip next 2 dc, 5 dc in next dc, skip next 2 dc, work
FPdc around next FPdc; repeat from ★ once **more**, dc in
last dc.
Finish off.
End Cap: With **right** side facing, using larger size hook,
and working in free loops of beginning ch **(Fig. 31b,
page 124)**, join Blue with slip st in first ch; ch 3, work
FPdc around next dc, ★ skip ch behind FPdc and next
2 chs, 5 dc in next ch, skip next 2 chs, work FPdc around
next dc; repeat from ★ once **more**, dc in next ch; finish off.

BORDER
Rnd 1: With **right** side facing, using larger size hook, and
working in end of rows, join Lt Blue with slip st in End
Cap; ch 3, (dc, ch 1, 2 dc) in same row, ch 1, (2 dc in next
row, ch 1) across to last row, (2 dc, ch 1) twice in last row,
skip first 4 sts on Row 99, ✝ (3 dc, ch 1, 3 dc) in next dc,
ch 1, skip next 2 dc, sc in next FPdc, ch 1, skip next 2 dc,
(3 dc, ch 1, 3 dc) in next dc, ch 1 ✝; working in end of
rows, (2 dc, ch 1) twice in first row, (2 dc in next row,
ch 1) across to End Cap, (2 dc, ch 1) twice in End Cap,
skip first 4 sts on End Cap, repeat from ✝ to ✝ once; join
with slip st to first dc, finish off: 434 sts.
Rnd 2: With **right** side facing and using smaller size hook,
join Blue with slip st in first ch-1 sp to left of last joining;
ch 1, sc in same sp, working in Back Loops Only (**Fig. 32,
page 124)**, ★ sc in each dc and in each ch-1 sp across to
next 3-dc group, sc in next 3 dc, 2 sc in next ch-1 sp, sc in
next 3 dc, skip next ch-1 sp and next sc, work FPdc around
FPdc in row **below** skipped sc, skip next ch-1 sp, sc in next
3 dc, 2 sc in next ch-1 sp, sc in next 3 dc and in next
ch-1 sp; repeat from ★ once **more**, sc in last 2 dc; join
with slip st to first sc: 648 sts.
Rnd 3: Ch 1, working in Back Loops Only, 3 sc in same st,
✝ sc in next 299 sc, 3 sc in next sc, sc in next 6 sc, 2 sc in
each of next 2 sc, sc in next 3 sc, skip next FPdc, sc in next
3 sc, 2 sc in each of next 2 sc, sc in next 6 sc ✝, 3 sc in next
sc, repeat from ✝ to ✝ once; join with slip st to first sc,
finish off.

ASSEMBLY
Place two Strips with **wrong** sides together and bottom
edges at the same end. Using Blue and working through
inside loops only, whipstitch Strips together, beginning in
center sc of first corner 3-sc group and ending in center sc
of next corner 3-sc group (**Fig. 33a, page 125**).

Join remaining Strips in same manner, always working in
same direction.

31

NOSTALGIC COVER-UP

This old-timey wrap is created with panels of light green V-stitches bordered by alternating rounds of off-white clusters and green puff stitches. The extra-wide strips are slip stitched together for easy assembly.

Finished Size: 53" x 70"

MATERIALS
Worsted Weight Yarn:
Lt Green - 22 ounces, (620 grams, 1,395 yards)
Off-White - 29 ounces, (820 grams, 1,840 yards)
Green - 13 ounces, (370 grams, 825 yards)
Crochet hook, size I (5.50 mm) **or** size needed for gauge

GAUGE: 12 dc and 6 rows = 4"
Each Strip = 7¹/₂" wide

STITCH GUIDE

V-ST
(Dc, ch 1, dc) in st or sp indicated.
BEGINNING CLUSTER
Ch 2, ★ YO, insert hook in same sp, YO and pull up a loop, YO and draw through 2 loops on hook; repeat from ★ once **more**, YO and draw through all 3 loops on hook *(Figs. 17a & b, page 120).*
CLUSTER
★ YO, insert hook in sp indicated, YO and pull up a loop, YO and draw through 2 loops on hook; repeat from ★ 2 times **more**, YO and draw through all 4 loops on hook.
PUFF ST
★ YO, insert hook in sp indicated, YO and pull up a loop even with loop on hook; repeat from ★ 3 times **more**, YO and draw through all 9 loops on hook *(Fig. 20, page 121).*

STRIP (Make 7)
CENTER
With Lt Green, ch 11 **loosely**.
Row 1 (Right side): Work V-St in fourth ch from hook, (skip next ch, work V-St in next ch) across to last ch, dc in last ch: 4 V-Sts.
Note: Loop a short piece of yarn around any stitch to mark Row 1 as **right** side and bottom edge.
Row 2: Ch 3 **(counts as first dc, now and throughout)**, turn; work V-St in each V-St (ch-1 sp) across, dc in top of beginning ch.
Rows 3-99: Ch 3, turn; work V-St in each V-St across, dc in last dc.
Finish off.

BORDER
Rnd 1: With **right** side facing and working in end of rows, join Off-White with slip st in last row; work (beginning Cluster, ch 3, Cluster) in same row, ch 1, (work Cluster in next row, ch 1) across to last row, work (Cluster, ch 3, Cluster) in last row, ch 1; working around beginning ch, (work Cluster in next ch-1 sp, ch 1) 3 times; working in end of rows, work (Cluster, ch 3, Cluster) in first row, ch 1, (work Cluster in next row, ch 1) across to last row, work (Cluster, ch 3, Cluster) in last row, ch 1; working across Row 99, skip first V-St, [work Cluster in sp **before** next V-St *(Fig. 27, page 122)*, ch 1] 3 times; join with slip st to top of beginning Cluster, finish off.
Rnd 2: With **wrong** side facing, join Green with slip st in any corner ch-3 sp; ch 1, work (Puff St, ch 5, Puff St) in same sp, ch 1, ★ † (work Puff St in next ch-1 sp, ch 1) across to next corner ch-3 sp †, work (Puff St, ch 5, Puff St) in corner sp, ch 1; repeat from ★ 2 times **more**, then repeat from † to † once; join with slip st to first st, finish off.
Rnd 3: With **right** side facing, join Off-White with slip st in any corner ch-5 sp; work beginning Cluster, ch 1, (work Cluster in same sp, ch 1) twice, (work Cluster in next ch-1 sp, ch 1) across to next corner ch-5 sp, ★ (work Cluster, ch 1) 3 times in corner sp, (work Cluster in next ch-1 sp, ch 1) across to next corner ch-5 sp; repeat from ★ 2 times **more**; join with slip st to top of beginning Cluster, finish off.

ASSEMBLY
Place two Strips with **right** sides together and bottom edges at the same end. Working through **both** pieces, join Off-White with slip st in center Cluster of top corner; ch 1, sc in same st and in next ch-1 sp, (ch 1, sc in next ch-1 sp) across to center Cluster of next corner, sc in center Cluster; finish off.

Join remaining Strips in same manner, always working in same direction.

FILIGREE FANTASY

Pamper yourself with a lacy blanket of soft golden clusters, double crochets, and chain spaces. The fancy filigree pattern lends a light, breezy touch to this heirloom wrap.

Finished Size: 47" x 63"

MATERIALS
Worsted Weight Yarn:
    51 ounces, (1,450 grams, 2,500 yards)
Crochet hook, size J (6.00 mm) **or** size needed for gauge

GAUGE: (3 sc, ch 3) twice = 3"
        Each Strip = 5¹/4" wide

STITCH GUIDE

> **DC DECREASE** (uses next 2 dc)
> ★ YO, insert hook in Back Loop Only of **next** dc, YO and pull up a loop, YO and draw through 2 loops on hook; repeat from ★ once **more**, YO and draw through all 3 loops on hook.
>
> **CLUSTER**
> ★ YO, insert hook in st or sp indicated, YO and pull up a loop, YO and draw through 2 loops on hook; repeat from ★ 2 times **more**, YO and draw through all 4 loops on hook *(Figs. 17a & b, page 120)*.
>
> **SC DECREASE** (uses next 2 Clusters)
> Pull up loop in Back Loop Only of next 2 Clusters, YO and draw through all 3 loops on hook **(counts as one sc)**.

FIRST STRIP
Ch 190 **loosely**.

Rnd 1 (Right side): 3 Sc in second ch from hook, ch 3, (skip next 2 chs, sc in next 3 chs, ch 3) across to last 3 chs, skip next 2 chs, 3 sc in last ch; working in free loops of beginning ch *(Fig. 31b, page 124)*, ch 3, skip next 2 chs, (sc in next 3 chs, ch 3, skip next 2 chs) across; join with slip st to first sc: 76 ch-3 sps.

Note: Loop a short piece of yarn around any stitch to mark Rnd 1 as **right** side.

Rnd 2: Slip st in next sc, ch 3 **(counts as first dc, now and throughout)**, dc in same st, (ch 1, 2 dc in same st) twice, ch 1, 3 sc in next ch-3 sp, ch 1, † skip next sc, (2 dc, ch 1) twice in next sc, 3 sc in next ch-3 sp, ch 1 †, repeat from † to † across to end 3-sc group, skip next sc, (2 dc, ch 1) 3 times in next sc, 3 sc in next ch-3 sp, ch 1, repeat from † to † across; join with slip st to first dc.

Rnd 3: Ch 2, dc in Back Loop Only of next dc *(Fig. 32, page 124)*, † ch 1, dc in next ch-1 sp, ch 1, (dc in Back Loop Only of next dc, ch 1) twice, dc in next ch-1 sp, ch 1, dc decrease, ch 3, skip next sc, sc in **both** loops of next sc, ch 3, ★ skip next ch-1 sp, work Cluster in next ch-1 sp, ch 3, skip next sc, sc in **both** loops of next sc, ch 3; repeat from ★ 36 times **more** †, dc decrease, repeat from † to † once; join with slip st to first dc: 74 Clusters.

Rnd 4: Slip st in first ch-1 sp, ch 1, sc in same sp, † ch 1, work (Cluster, ch 1) twice in next ch-1 sp, working in both loops, [sc in next dc, ch 1, (work Cluster, ch 1) twice in next ch-1 sp] twice, sc in next ch-1 sp, ch 3, sc in next ch-3 sp, ch 1, work (Cluster, ch 1) twice in next sc, ★ sc in next 2 ch-3 sps, ch 1, (work Cluster, ch 1) twice in next sc; repeat from ★ 36 times **more**, sc in next ch-3 sp, ch 3 †, sc in next ch-1 sp, repeat from † to † once; join with slip st to first sc: 164 Clusters.

Rnd 5: Ch 3, 2 dc in **both** loops of same st, † ch 1, (sc decrease, ch 1, 3 dc in **both** loops of next sc, ch 1) 3 times, sc in next ch-3 sp, ch 1, sc decrease, ch 1, ★ (dc in **both** loops of next sc, ch 1) twice, sc decrease, ch 1; repeat from ★ 36 times **more**, sc in next ch-3 sp, ch 1 †, 3 dc in **both** loops of next sc, repeat from † to † once; join with slip st to first dc.

Rnd 6: Working in **both** loops, slip st in next dc, ch 3, slip st in same st, † ch 1, (2 dc, ch 2, 2 dc) in next sc, ch 1, skip next dc, (slip st, ch 3, slip st) in next dc, ch 1, [dc, (ch 1, tr) twice] in next sc, ch 3, [(tr, ch 1) twice, dc] in same st, ch 1, skip next dc, (slip st, ch 3, slip st) in next dc, ch 1, (2 dc, ch 2, 2 dc) in next sc, ch 1, skip next dc, (slip st, ch 3, slip st) in next dc, ch 3, slip st in next sc, ch 1, (2 dc, ch 2, 2 dc) in next sc, ch 1, ★ skip next ch-1 sp, (slip st, ch 3, slip st) in next ch-1 sp, ch 1, (2 dc, ch 2, 2 dc) in next sc, ch 1; repeat from ★ 36 times **more**, slip st in next sc, ch 3 †, skip next dc, (slip st, ch 3, slip st) in next dc, repeat from † to † once; join with slip st to first slip st, finish off.

REMAINING 8 STRIPS

Work same as First Strip through Rnd 5.

Rnd 6 (Joining rnd)**:** Working in **both** loops, slip st in next dc, ch 3, slip st in same st, † ch 1, (2 dc, ch 2, 2 dc) in next sc, ch 1, skip next dc, (slip st, ch 3, slip st) in next dc, ch 1, [dc, (ch 1, tr) twice] in next sc, ch 3, [(tr, ch 1) twice, dc] in same st, ch 1, skip next dc, (slip st, ch 3, slip st) in next dc, ch 1, (2 dc, ch 2, 2 dc) in next sc, ch 1, skip next dc, (slip st, ch 3, slip st) in next dc, ch 3, slip st in next sc, ch 1 †, (2 dc, ch 2, 2 dc) in next sc, ch 1, [skip next ch-1 sp, (slip st, ch 3, slip st) in next ch-1 sp, ch 1, (2 dc, ch 2, 2 dc) in next sc, ch 1] 37 times, slip st in next sc,

ch 3, skip next dc, (slip st, ch 3, slip st) in next dc, repeat from † to † once, holding Strips with **wrong** sides together, 2 dc in next sc, ch 1, slip st in corresponding ch-2 sp on **previous Strip (Fig. 28, page 122)**, ch 1, 2 dc in same st on **new Strip**, ch 1, ★ skip next ch-1 sp, (slip st, ch 3, slip st) in next ch-1 sp, ch 1, 2 dc in next sc, ch 1, slip st in corresponding ch-2 sp on **previous Strip**, ch 1, 2 dc in same st on **new Strip**, ch 1; repeat from ★ 36 times **more**, slip st in next sc, ch 3; join with slip st to first slip st, finish off.

CROWNING BEAUTY

This blanket of crown shell stitches is a picture of casual elegance. Worked in four-inch-wide strips, the stylish throw is finished with a beautiful scalloped edging.

Finished Size: 44" x 60"

MATERIALS
Worsted Weight Yarn:
45¹/₂ ounces, (1,300 grams, 2,990 yards)
Crochet hook, size I (5.50 mm) **or** size needed for gauge

GAUGE: In pattern, (sc, ch 2) 6 times = 4"
Each Strip = 4" wide

FIRST STRIP
Ch 260 **loosely**.
Rnd 1 (Right side): Working in top 2 loops of each ch *(Fig. 2b, page 116)*, (sc, ch 2) 3 times in second ch from hook, skip next 2 chs, (sc in next ch, ch 2, skip next 2 chs) across to last ch, (sc, ch 2) 3 times in last ch; working in free loops of beginning ch *(Fig. 31b, page 124)*, skip next 2 chs, (sc in next ch, ch 2, skip next 2 chs) across; join with slip st to first sc: 176 sc.
Rnd 2: Ch 1, sc in same st, 7 dc in next sc, sc in next sc, (5 dc in next sc, sc in next sc) 43 times, 7 dc in next sc, (sc in next sc, 5 dc in next sc) across; join with slip st to first sc.
To work **Back Post half double crochet (abbreviated BPhdc)**, YO, insert hook from **back** to **front** around post of next dc, YO and pull up a loop *(Fig. 14, page 119)*, YO and draw through all 3 loops on hook. Skip st in front of BPhdc.
Rnd 3: Ch 3, 6 dc in Back Loop Only of same st *(Fig. 32, page 124)*, † ch 1, skip next 3 dc, work BPhdc around next dc, ch 1, skip next 3 dc, 7 dc in Back Loop Only of next sc, skip next 2 dc, work BPhdc around next dc, skip next 2 dc, (5 dc in Back Loop Only of next sc, skip next 2 dc, work BPhdc around next dc) 42 times, skip next 2 dc †, 7 dc in Back Loop Only of next sc, repeat from † to † once; join with slip st to top of beginning ch-3.

To **decrease**, insert hook from **front** to **back** in next dc, skip next dc and insert hook from **back** to **front** in next dc *(Fig. 21, page 121)*, YO and pull up a loop, YO and draw through both loops on hook.
Rnd 4: Slip st in next dc, ch 1, ★ decrease, ch 2, (sc, ch 3, sc) in next ch-1 sp, 5 hdc in next BPhdc, (sc, ch 3, sc) in next ch-1 sp, ch 2, skip next 2 dc, decrease, ch 2, (sc, ch 3, sc) in next BPhdc, [ch 2, skip next dc, decrease, ch 2, (sc, ch 3, sc) in next BPhdc] 42 times, ch 2, skip next 2 dc; repeat from ★ once **more**; join with slip st to first decrease, finish off.

REMAINING 10 STRIPS
Work same as First Strip through Rnd 3.
Rnd 4 (Joining rnd): Slip st in next dc, ch 1, decrease, ch 2, (sc, ch 3, sc) in next ch-1 sp, 5 hdc in next BPhdc, (sc, ch 3, sc) in next ch-1 sp, ch 2, skip next 2 dc, decrease, ch 2, (sc, ch 3, sc) in next BPhdc, [ch 2, skip next dc, decrease, ch 2, (sc, ch 3, sc) in next BPhdc] 42 times, ch 2, skip next 2 dc, decrease, ch 2, (sc, ch 3, sc) in next ch-1 sp, 5 hdc in next BPhdc, (sc, ch 3, sc) in next ch-1 sp, ch 2, skip next 2 dc, decrease, ch 2, sc in next BPhdc, ch 1, holding Strips with **wrong** sides together, slip st in corresponding ch-3 sp on **previous** Strip *(Fig. 28, page 122)*, ch 1, sc in same st on **new** Strip, ★ ch 2, skip next dc, decrease, ch 2, sc in next BPhdc, ch 1, slip st in next ch-3 sp on **previous** Strip, ch 1, sc in same st on **new** Strip; repeat from ★ 41 times **more**, ch 2, skip next 2 dc; join with slip st to first decrease, finish off.

BUTTERFLY BLUES

Let your imagination soar and you'll find a field of fluttering butterflies on this captivating afghan! Blue borders of post stitches and double crochets surround the outstretched wings of the ecru wonders.

Finished Size: 52" x 71"

MATERIALS
Worsted Weight Yarn:
  Ecru - 21 ounces, (600 grams, 1,225 yards)
  Lt Blue - 34 ounces, (970 grams, 1,985 yards)
  Blue - 21 ounces, (600 grams, 1,225 yards)
Crochet hook, size J (6.00 mm) **or** size needed for gauge
Yarn needle

GAUGE: 14 dc = 4"
  Each Strip = 3¹/4" wide

STRIP (Make 16)
CENTER
With Ecru, ch 238 **loosely**.
Row 1 (Right side): Dc in fourth ch from hook **(3 skipped chs count as first dc)** and in each ch across; finish off: 236 dc.
Note: Loop a short piece of yarn around first dc to mark Row 1 as **right** side and bottom edge.
Row 2: With **right** side facing, join Lt Blue with slip st in first dc; ch 3 **(counts as first dc, now and throughout)**, dc in next dc and in each dc across; finish off.
Row 3: With **right** side facing, join Ecru with slip st in first dc; ch 3, dc in next dc and in each dc across; finish off.

BORDER
To work **Front Post treble crochet (abbreviated FPtr)**, YO twice, insert hook from **front** to **back** around post of st indicated, YO and pull up a loop **(Fig. 12, page 118)**, (YO and draw through 2 loops on hook) 3 times. Skip st behind FPtr.
Rnd 1: With **right** side facing, join Blue with slip st in first dc; ch 1, sc in same st and in next 2 dc, † skip next st, work FPtr around dc on Row 2 **below** next st, work FPtr around dc on Row 2 **below** skipped st, ★ sc in next 2 sts, skip next st, work FPtr around dc on Row 2 **below** next st, work FPtr around dc on Row 2 **below** skipped st; repeat from ★ across to last 3 sts, sc in last 3 sts; working in end of rows, (sc, hdc, dc) in first row, 5 tr in next row, (dc, hdc, sc) in last row †; working in free loops of beginning ch **(Fig. 31b, page 124)**, sc in first 3 chs, repeat from † to † once; join with slip st to first sc, finish off: 494 sts.

To work **Front Post half double crochet (abbreviated FPhdc)**, YO, insert hook from **front** to **back** around post of st indicated, YO and pull up a loop **(Fig. 10, page 118)**, YO and draw through all 3 loops on hook. Skip st behind FPhdc.
Rnd 2: With **right** side facing and working in Back Loops Only **(Fig. 32, page 124)**, join Lt Blue with slip st in same st as joining; ch 1, sc in same st and in next 2 sc, † work FPhdc around each of next 2 FPtr, ★ sc in next 2 sc, work FPhdc around each of next 2 FPtr; repeat from ★ across to last 4 sc on same side, sc in last 4 sc and in next 2 sts, 2 sc in next tr, work FPhdc around each of next 3 tr, 2 sc in next tr †, sc in next 6 sts, repeat from † to † once, sc in last 3 sts; join with slip st to Back Loop Only of first sc: 498 sts.
Rnd 3: Ch 1, working in Back Loops Only, 2 sc in same st, place marker around last sc made for joining placement, † sc each st across to last FPhdc on same side, sc in last FPhdc and in next 3 sc, place marker around last sc made for joining placement, sc in same st and in next sc †, 2 sc in next sc, (sc in next st, 2 sc in next st) 6 times, place marker around last sc made for joining placement, repeat from † to † once, (2 sc in next st, sc in next st) 6 times; join with slip st to both loops of first sc, finish off.

ASSEMBLY
Place two Strips with **wrong** sides together and bottom edges at the same end. Using Lt Blue and working through inside loops only, whipstitch Strips together, beginning in first marked sc and ending in next marked sc **(Fig. 33a, page 125)**.

Join remaining Strips in same manner, always working in the same direction.

AROUND WE GO!

Worked in luxurious shades of rose and taupe, interlocking rings of double crochets create this heirloom wrap. A scalloped border gives the enchanting afghan a feeling of yesteryear.

Finished Size: 48" x 63"

MATERIALS
Worsted Weight Yarn:
Dk Rose - 32 ounces, (910 grams, 2,085 yards)
Rose - 10½ ounces, (300 grams, 685 yards)
Taupe - 18 ounces, (510 grams, 1,175 yards)
Crochet hook, size J (6.00 mm) **or** size needed for gauge

GAUGE: 3 rings = 5" long
Center = 2¼" wide
Each Strip = 6" wide

STRIP (Make 8)
CENTER
FIRST RING
With Rose, ch 13; join with slip st to form a ring.
Rnd 1 (Right side): Ch 3 **(counts as first dc, now and throughout)**, 27 dc in ring; join with slip st to first dc, finish off: 28 dc.
Note: Loop a short piece of yarn around any stitch to mark Rnd 1 as **right** side.
SECOND RING
With Dk Rose, ch 13, with **wrong** side of previous ring facing, insert end of beginning ch-13 through center of previous ring; join with slip st to form a ring.
Rnd 1 (Right side): Ch 3, 27 dc in ring; join with slip st to first dc, finish off: 28 dc.
Note: Mark Rnd 1 as **right** side.
REMAINING 47 RINGS
Work same as Second Ring in following Color Sequence:
Taupe, Rose, ★ Dk Rose, Taupe, Rose; repeat from ★ 14 times **more**.

BORDER
Note: Work into Rings with **right** side of each Ring facing at all times.
Rnd 1: With **right** side facing, join Taupe with slip st in any dc on First Ring; ch 3, dc in same st and in next dc, 2 dc in next dc, ch 1, skip next dc, dc in next 4 dc, (ch 1, dc in any 4 consecutive dc on next ring) 48 times, ch 1, skip next dc, 2 dc in next dc, (dc in next dc, 2 dc in next dc) 5 times, ch 1, skip next dc, dc in next 4 dc, (ch 1, skip next 10 dc on next ring, dc in next 4 dc) across to last ring,

ch 1, skip next 7 dc on last ring, dc in next 4 dc, ch 1, skip next dc, (2 dc in next dc, dc in next dc) 4 times; join with slip st to first dc, finish off: 426 dc.
Rnd 2: With **right** side facing, join Dk Rose with slip st in first dc to left of last joining; ch 1, sc in same st and in each dc and each ch-1 sp across to last ch-1 sp on same side, sc in ch-1 sp and in next 5 dc, sc in sp **before** next dc (*Fig. 27, page 122*) and in next 7 dc, sc in sp **before** next dc and in each dc and ch-1 sp across to last ch-1 sp, sc in last ch-1 sp and in next 5 dc, sc in sp **before** next dc and in next 7 dc, sc in sp **before** next dc and in last dc; join with slip st to Back Loop Only of first sc (*Fig. 32, page 124*): 530 sc.
To work **double treble crochet (abbreviated dtr)**, YO 3 times, insert hook in st or sp indicated, YO and pull up a loop, (YO and draw through 2 loops on hook) 4 times (*Figs. 8a & b, page 117*).
Rnd 3: Ch 1, working in Back Loops Only, sc in same st, † skip next sc, (dc, tr, ch 1, tr, dc) in next sc, skip next sc, sc in next sc, ★ skip next sc, (dc, tr) in next sc, ch 1, (tr, dc) in next sc, skip next sc, sc in next sc; repeat from ★ 48 times **more**, skip next sc, (dc, tr, ch 1, tr, dc) in next sc, skip next sc, sc in next sc, skip next sc, 5 dc in next sc, skip next sc, sc in next sc, skip next sc, (2 dc, tr, 2 dtr, tr, 2 dc) in next sc, skip next sc, sc in next sc, skip next sc, 5 dc in next sc, skip next sc †, sc in next sc, repeat from † to † once; join with slip st to **both** loops of first sc, finish off.

TRIM
FIRST SIDE
Row 1: With **wrong** side facing, join Dk Rose with slip st in first ch-1 sp on either side; ch 1, sc in same sp, (ch 4, sc in next ch-1 sp) across: 50 ch-4 sps.
Row 2: Ch 1, turn; sc in each sc and in each ch across; finish off.
SECOND SIDE
Work same as First Side.

ASSEMBLY
Place two Strips with **wrong** sides together. Using Dk Rose and working through inside loops only, whipstitch Strips together, beginning in first sc of Trim and ending in last sc (*Fig. 33a, page 125*).

Join remaining Strips in same manner, always working in same direction.

AZTEC TOUCH

Teal, rust, and black yarns give this unique wrap an Aztec touch. The bold pattern is created by working center strips of narrow color-blocked rows and then adding the eye-catching border rounds.

Finished Size: 45½" x 64"

MATERIALS

Teal - 18 ounces, (510 grams, 1,175 yards)
Rust - 14 ounces, (400 grams, 915 yards)
Black - 11 ounces, (310 grams, 720 yards)
Crochet hook, size G (4.00 mm) **or** size needed for gauge
Yarn needle

GAUGE: Center = 1¾" wide and 8 rows = 4¼"
Each Strip = 3½" wide

STRIP (Make 13)
CENTER

With Rust, ch 9 **loosely**.

Row 1 (Right side): Dc in fourth ch from hook **(3 skipped chs count as first dc)** and in each ch across: 7 dc.

Note: Loop a short piece of yarn around any stitch to mark Row 1 as **right** side and bottom edge.

Rows 2 and 3: Ch 3, turn; dc in next dc and in each dc across.

Row 4: Ch 3, turn; dc in next dc and in each dc across changing to Teal in last dc *(Fig. 30a, page 124)*.

Rows 5-7: Ch 3, turn; dc in next dc and in each dc across.

Row 8: Ch 3, turn; dc in next dc and in each dc across changing to Rust in last dc.

Rows 9-11: Ch 3, turn; dc in next dc and in each dc across.

Rows 12-115: Repeat Rows 4-11, 13 times.

Row 116: Ch 3, turn; dc in next dc and in each dc across; finish off.

BORDER

To work **Front Post treble crochet (abbreviated FPtr)**, YO twice, insert hook from **front** to **back** around post of st indicated, YO and pull up a loop *(Fig. 12, page 118)*, (YO and draw through 2 loops on hook) 3 times.

Rnd 1: With **right** side facing and working in end of rows, join Black with slip st in last row; ch 3, 2 dc in same row, skip next row, working in **front** of first dc, tr around second dc on next row, working in **front** of tr just made, tr around second dc on skipped row, † 3 dc in each of next 2 rows, skip next row, working in **front** of first dc, tr around second dc on next row, working in **front** of tr just made, tr around second dc on skipped row †, repeat from † to † 27 times **more**, 3 dc in last row; working in free loops of beginning ch *(Fig. 31b, page 124)*, skip first 3 chs, 3 tr in next ch, work FPtr around dc **below** same ch, 3 tr in same ch; working in end of rows, 3 dc in first row, skip next row, working in **front** of first dc, tr around second dc on next row, working in **front** of tr just made, tr around second dc on skipped row, repeat from † to † 28 times, 3 dc in last row; working across last row, skip first 3 dc, 3 tr in next dc, work FPtr around same dc, 3 tr in same dc; with Teal, join with slip st to first dc: 478 sts.

Rnd 2: Ch 1, sc in same st, place marker around last sc made for joining placement, sc in next 231 sts, place marker around last sc worked for joining placement, 2 sc in each of next 7 sts, sc in next dc, place marker around last sc made for joining placement, sc in each st across to last 7 sts, place marker around last sc made for joining placement, 2 sc in each of last 7 sts; join with slip st to first sc, finish off.

ASSEMBLY

Place two Strips with **wrong** sides together and bottom edges at the same end. Using Teal and working through inside loops only, whipstitch Strips together, beginning in first marked sc and ending in next marked sc *(Fig. 33a, page 125)*.

Join remaining Strips in same manner, always working in same direction.

BLACK TIE-WHITE TIE

For an evening of refined relaxation, wrap yourself in our sophisticated throw. Treble and double crochets form black and white "bow ties" down the center of each strip, and the woven-look edging is created by pulling white chain loops through black chain spaces.

Finished Size: 46¹/₂" x 61"

MATERIALS
Worsted Weight Yarn:
  Black - 18 ounces, (510 grams, 1,020 yards)
  White - 10 ounces, (280 grams, 565 yards)
  Gray - 12 ounces, (340 grams, 680 yards)
Crochet hook, size G (4.00 mm) **or** size needed for gauge

GAUGE: Center = 2" wide and 4 rows (2 repeats) = 2¹/₄"
    Each Strip = 4" wide

FIRST STRIP
CENTER
With Black, ch 10 **loosely**.
Row 1 (Right side): Tr in fifth ch from hook **(4 skipped chs count as first tr)**, dc in next ch, slip st around next ch, dc in next ch, tr in last 2 chs: 7 sts.
Note: Loop a short piece of yarn around any stitch to mark Row 1 as **right** side and bottom edge.
Row 2: Ch 6, turn; skip first 6 sts, slip st in last tr.
Row 3: Ch 4 **(counts as first tr, now and throughout)**, turn; tr in next ch, dc in next ch, slip st around next ch, dc in next ch, tr in last 2 chs: 7 sts.
Rows 4-101: Repeat Rows 2 and 3, 49 times.
Finish off.

BORDER
Rnd 1: With **right** side facing, join White with sc in last tr made *(see Joining With Sc, page 124)*; sc in same st, † working in end of rows, 3 sc in first row, (sc in next sp, 3 sc in next row) across † ; working in free loops of beginning ch *(Fig. 31b, page 124)*, 3 sc in first ch, ch 3, skip next 5 chs, 3 sc in next ch, repeat from † to † once, 3 sc in first tr, ch 3, skip next 5 sts, sc in same st as first sc; join with slip st to first sc, finish off: 418 sc and 2 ch-3 sps.
Rnd 2: With **right** side facing, join Gray with slip st in same st as last joining; ch 3, dc in same st and in each sc across to center sc of next corner 3-sc group, † 3 dc in center sc, dc in next sc, 5 dc in next ch-3 sp, dc in next sc †, 3 dc in next sc, dc in next sc and in each sc across to center sc of next corner 3-sc group, repeat from † to † once, dc in same st as beginning ch-3; join with slip st to top of beginning ch-3, finish off: 436 sts.

Rnd 3: With **right** side facing, join Black with sc in same st as last joining; ch 2, skip next dc, sc in next dc, place marker around last ch-2 made for joining placement, (ch 2, skip next dc, sc in next dc) 103 times, place marker around last ch-2 made for joining placement, (ch 2, skip next dc, sc in next dc) around, ch 2, skip last dc; join with slip st to first sc, finish off.

SECOND STRIP
CENTER
With White work same as First Strip.

BORDER
Rnd 1: With Black, work same as First Strip.
Rnd 2: Work same as First Strip.
Rnd 3 (Joining rnd): With **right** side facing, join Black with sc in same st as last joining; ch 2, skip next dc, sc in next dc, place marker around last ch-2 made for joining placement, (ch 2, skip next dc, sc in next dc) 103 times, place marker around last ch-2 made for joining placement, (ch 2, skip next sc, sc in next dc) 5 times, ch 1, holding Strips with **wrong** sides together and bottom edges at same end, slip st in first marked ch-2 sp on **previous Strip** *(Fig. 28, page 122)*, ch 1, skip next dc on **new Strip**, sc in next dc, ★ ch 1, slip st in next ch-2 sp on **previous Strip**, ch 1, skip next dc on **new Strip**, sc in next dc; repeat from ★ 102 times **more**, (ch 2, skip next dc, sc in next dc) around, ch 2, skip last dc; join with slip st to first sc, finish off.

THIRD STRIP
Work same as First Strip through Rnd 2 of Border.
Rnd 3: Work same as Second Strip.

REMAINING 8 STRIPS
Repeat Second and Third Strips, 4 times.

EDGING
Rnd 1: With **right** side facing, join Black with sc in any ch-2 sp; ch 3, (sc in next ch-2 sp, ch 3) around; join with slip st to first sc, finish off.
Rnd 2: With **right** side facing, join White with slip st in any ch-3 sp; ★ ch 4, drop loop from hook, insert hook from **front** to **back** in next ch-3 sp, hook dropped loop and pull through; repeat from ★ around; join with slip st to first slip st, finish off.

EARLY-AMERICAN SPIRIT

A salute to our forefathers' all-American spirit, this provincial throw is worked in traditional Colonial colors. Each row features crisscrossing post stitches of ruby red surrounded by creamy double crochets and blue cluster stitches.

Finished Size: 47" x 63"

MATERIALS
Worsted Weight Yarn:
   Red - 21 ounces, (600 grams, 1,190 yards)
   Off-White - 19 ounces, (540 grams, 1,075 yards)
   Blue - 23 ounces, (650 grams, 1,300 yards)
Crochet hook, size H (5.00 mm) **or** size needed for gauge
Yarn needle

GAUGE: Center = 1³/₄" wide and 10 rows = 4"
          Each Strip = 5¹/₄" wide

STITCH GUIDE

FRONT POST DOUBLE TREBLE CROCHET
   (abbreviated FPdtr)
YO 3 times, insert hook from **front** to **back** around post of st indicated, YO and pull up a loop *(Fig. 13, page 119)*, (YO and draw through 2 loops on hook) 4 times.

CLUSTER
★ YO, insert hook in st indicated, YO and pull up a loop, YO and draw through 2 loops on hook; repeat from ★ 2 times **more**, YO and draw through all 4 loops on hook *(Figs. 17a & b, page 120)*.

FRONT POST DOUBLE CROCHET
   (abbreviated FPdc)
YO, insert hook from **front** to **back** around post of st indicated, YO and pull up a loop *(Fig. 11, page 118)*, (YO and draw through 2 loops on hook) twice. Skip st behind FPdc .

STRIP (Make 9)
CENTER
With Red, ch 6; join with slip st to form a ring.
Row 1: Ch 3 **(counts as first dc, now and throughout)**, 5 dc in ring: 6 dc.
Note: Loop a short piece of yarn around any stitch to mark Row 1 as **right** side and bottom edge.
Row 2: Ch 1, turn; sc in each dc across.
Row 3: Ch 3, turn; work FPdtr around fifth dc on Row 1, dc in sc behind FPdtr and in next 3 sc, work FPdtr around third dc on Row 1 to right of last FPdtr made, dc in last sc: 8 sts.
Row 4: Ch 1, turn; sc in first dc, skip next FPdtr, sc in next 4 dc, skip next FPdtr, sc in last dc: 6 sc.

Row 5: Ch 3, turn; work FPdtr around second FPdtr 2 rows **below**, dc in sc behind FPdtr and in next 3 sc, work FPdtr around first FPdtr 2 rows **below**, dc in last sc.
Rows 6-135: Repeat Rows 4 and 5, 65 times.
Row 136: Ch 1, turn; pull up a loop in first dc, skip next FPdtr, pull up a loop in next dc, YO and draw through all 3 loops on hook, pull up a loop in next 2 dc, YO and draw through all 3 loops on hook, pull up a loop in next dc, skip next FPdtr, pull up a loop in last dc, YO and draw through all 3 loops on hook: 3 sts.
Row 137: Ch 4, turn; skip first 2 sts, slip st in last st; finish off.

BORDER
Rnd 1: With **right** side facing, join Off-White with slip st in last ch-4 sp; ch 4 **(counts as first tr)**, 10 tr in same sp; working in end of rows, (skip next sc row, 3 dc in next dc row) across to beginning ring, 11 tr in ring; working in end of rows, 3 dc in first dc row, (skip next sc row, 3 dc in next dc row) across to last sc row, skip last sc row; join with slip st to first tr: 68 3-dc groups **each** side.
Rnd 2: Ch 3, working in Back Loops Only *(Fig. 32, page 124)*, dc in same st and in next tr, 2 dc in next tr, dc in next tr, 2 dc in each of next 3 tr, (dc in next tr, 2 dc in next tr) twice, dc in each dc across to next 11-tr group, (2 dc in next tr, dc in next tr) twice, 2 dc in each of next 3 tr, (dc in next tr, 2 dc in next tr) twice, dc in each dc across; join with slip st to first dc, finish off: 444 dc.
Rnd 3: With **right** side facing and working in both loops, join Blue with slip st in same st as last joining; ch 1, sc in same st and in next dc, work Cluster in free loop on Rnd 1 below next dc *(Fig. 31a, page 124)*, † skip dc behind Cluster, sc in next 2 dc, work Cluster in free loop **below** next dc, skip dc behind Cluster, sc in next 3 dc, work Cluster in free loop **below** same st, do **not** skip dc behind Cluster, sc in next 3 dc, work Cluster in free loop **below** next dc, skip dc behind Cluster, sc in next 2 dc, work Cluster in free loop **below** next dc, skip dc behind Cluster, sc in next 3 dc, work Cluster in free loop **below** next dc, ★ skip dc behind Cluster, sc in next 2 dc, work Cluster in free loop **below** next dc; repeat from ★ 66 times **more** †, skip dc behind Cluster, sc in next 3 dc, work Cluster in free loop **below** next dc, repeat from † to † once, skip dc behind Cluster, sc in last dc; join with slip st to first sc: 146 Clusters.

Rnd 4: Ch 3, † place marker around last dc made for joining placement, dc in next sc, work FPdc around next Cluster, 2 dc in each of next 2 sc, work FPdc around next Cluster, (2 dc in each of next 3 sc, work FPdc around next Cluster) twice, 2 dc in each of next 2 sc, work FPdc around next Cluster, dc in next 2 sc, place marker around last dc made for joining placement, dc in next sc, work FPdc around next Cluster, (dc in next 2 sc, work FPdc around next Cluster) 67 times †, dc in next 2 sc, repeat from † to † once, dc in last sc; join with slip st to first dc, finish off.

Trim: With **right** side facing, using Red, and holding working yarn on **wrong** side, insert hook in sp **between** any 2 dc on Rnd 4 and pull up a loop *(Fig, 27, page 122)*, ★ insert hook in sp **before** next dc, YO and draw **loosely** through sp and loop on hook; repeat from ★ around; join with slip st to first st, finish off.

ASSEMBLY

Place two Strip with **wrong** sides together and bottom edges at the same end. Using Blue and working through inside loops only, whipstitch Strips together, beginning in first marked dc and ending in next marked dc *(Fig. 33a, page 125)*.

Join remaining Strips in same manner, always working in same direction.

SUNNY SCALLOPS

*Sunny scallops fashioned with single and double crochets
are set off by simple white stitches on this blanket for baby.
A classic filet edging completes the cheery cover-up.*

Finished Size: 35" x 46"

MATERIALS
Sport Weight Yarn:
  Blue - 8 ounces, (230 grams, 755 yards)
  Yellow - 8 ounces, (230 grams, 755 yards)
  White - 3 ounces, (90 grams, 285 yards)
Crochet hook, size G (4.00 mm) **or** size needed for gauge
Yarn needle

GAUGE: In pattern, sc, (ch 1, sc) 4 times = 2"
       Each Strip = 3¼" wide

STRIP (Make 10)
FIRST SIDE
With Yellow, ch 200 **loosely**.

Row 1 (Right side): Sc in second ch from hook and in next ch, ch 1, ★ skip next ch, sc in next ch, ch 1; repeat from ★ across to last 3 chs, skip next ch, sc in last 2 chs: 101 sc and 98 ch-1 sps.

Note: Loop a short piece of yarn around any stitch to mark Row 1 as **right** side.

Row 2: Ch 1, turn; sc in first 2 sc, ch 1, skip next sc, (dc, ch 1) 3 times in next ch-1 sp, ★ skip next sc, (sc in next sc, ch 1) 3 times, skip next sc, (dc, ch 1) 3 times in next ch-1 sp; repeat from ★ across to last 3 sc, skip next sc, sc in last 2 sc: 121 sts and 118 ch-1 sps.

Row 3: Ch 1, turn; sc in first sc, ch 1, skip next sc, dc in next dc, ch 1, (dc in next ch-1 sp, ch 1, dc in next dc, ch 1) twice, ★ skip next sc, (sc in next ch-1 sp, ch 1) twice, dc in next dc, ch 1, (dc in next ch-1 sp, ch 1, dc in next dc, ch 1) twice; repeat from ★ across to last 2 sc, skip next sc, sc in last sc; finish off: 140 sts and 139 ch-1 sps.

Row 4: With **wrong** side facing, join White with sc in first sc *(see Joining With Sc, page 124)*; (ch 1, sc in next dc) 5 times, ★ ch 2, skip next ch-1 sp, working **behind** next ch-1, slip st in sc one row **below** ch-1, ch 2, sc in next dc, (ch 1, sc in next dc) 4 times; repeat from ★ across to last sc, ch 1, sc in last sc; finish off: 121 sts and 120 sps.

To work **double treble crochet** *(abbreviated dtr)*, YO 3 times, insert hook in sp indicated, YO and pull up a loop, (YO and draw through 2 loops on hook) 4 times *(Figs. 8a & b, page 117)*.

Row 5: With **right** side facing, join Blue with slip st in first sc; ch 4 **(counts as first tr, now and throughout)**, dc in next sc, ch 1, hdc in next sc, ch 1, sc in next sc, ch 1, hdc in next sc, ch 1, dc in next sc, ★ dtr in ch-1 sp **behind** next slip st, dc in next sc, ch 1, hdc in next sc, ch 1, sc in next sc, ch 1, hdc in next sc, ch 1, dc in next sc; repeat from ★ across to last sc, tr in last sc: 121 sts and 80 sps.

Row 6: Ch 1, turn; sc in first 2 sts, ch 1, ★ (skip next ch-1 sp, sc in next st, ch 1) 4 times, skip next dtr, sc in next dc, ch 1; repeat from ★ 18 times **more**, (skip next ch-1 sp, sc in next st, ch 1) 3 times, skip next ch-1 sp, sc in last 2 sts; finish off: 102 sc and 99 ch-1 sps.

SECOND SIDE
Row 1: With **wrong** side facing and working in free loops of beginning ch *(Fig. 31b, page 124)*, join Yellow with sc in ch at base of first sc; sc in next ch, ch 1, skip next 2 chs, (dc, ch 1) 3 times in next ch-1 sp (same sp as 3-dc group on First Side), ★ skip next 2 chs, sc in next ch, ch 1, (skip next ch, sc in next ch, ch 1) twice, skip next 2 chs, (dc, ch 1) 3 times in next ch-1 sp (same sp as 3-dc group on First Side); repeat from ★ across to last 4 chs, skip next 2 chs, sc in last 2 chs: 121 sts and 118 ch-1 sps.

Rows 2-5: Work same as Rows 3-6 of First Side.

ASSEMBLY
Place two Strips with **wrong** sides together. Using Blue and working through both loops, whipstitch Strips together, beginning in first sc and ending in last sc *(Fig. 33b, page 125)*.

EDGING
Rnd 1: With **right** side facing and working across one long edge, join Blue with sc in first sc; ch 2, sc in same st, † ch 1, (sc in next ch-1 sp, ch 1) across to last 2 sc, skip next sc, (sc, ch 2, sc) in last sc, ch 1; (sc, ch 1) evenly across end of rows †; working across opposite long edge, (sc, ch 2, sc) in first sc, repeat from † to † once; join with slip st to first sc.

Rnd 2: Turn; slip st in first ch-1 sp, ch 1, sc in same sp, ch 1, ★ (sc in next ch-1 sp, ch 1) across to next corner ch-2 sp, (sc, ch 2, sc) in corner ch-2 sp, ch 1; repeat from ★ around; join with slip st to first sc.

Rnd 3: Turn; slip st in first ch-1 sp, ch 4 **(counts as first dc plus ch 1)**, (dc, ch 3, dc) in next ch-2 sp, ch 1, ★ (dc in next ch-1 sp, ch 1) across to next corner ch-2 sp, (dc, ch 3, dc) in corner ch-2 sp, ch 1; repeat from ★ 2 times **more**, (dc in next ch-1 sp, ch 1) across; join with slip st to first dc.

Rnd 4: Ch 1, do **not** turn; sc in same st, ch 1, sc in next dc, ch 1, (sc, ch 1) 3 times in next ch-3 sp, ★ (sc in next dc, ch 1) across to next corner ch-3 sp, (sc, ch 1) 3 times in corner ch-3 sp; repeat from ★ 2 times **more**, (sc in next dc, ch 1) across; join with slip st to first sc.

Rnd 5: Slip st in first ch-1 sp, ch 1, (slip st in next ch-1 sp, ch 1) around; join with slip st to first slip st, finish off.

HOLLY GARLAND

Showcasing a garland of holly and French-knot "berries," our unique throw is a happy addition to the holidays. The glad tidings afghan works up easily, so it's a terrific project for beginners!

Finished Size: 49¹/₂" x 64¹/₂"

MATERIALS
Worsted Weight Yarn:
Green - 18 ounces, (510 grams, 1,135 yards)
Tan - 22 ounces, (620 grams, 1,385 yards)
Red - 9 ounces, (260 grams, 570 yards)
Crochet hook, size G (4.00 mm) **or** size needed for gauge

GAUGE: Each Holly Leaf = 1³/₄" x 2¹/₂"
Each Strip = 4¹/₂" wide

FIRST STRIP
CENTER
Row 1 (Right side): With Green, ch 2, 3 sc in second ch from hook.
Note: Loop a short piece of yarn around any stitch to mark Row 1 as **right** side and bottom edge.
Row 2: Ch 1, turn; sc in each sc across.
Row 3: Ch 1, turn; 2 sc in first sc, sc in next sc, 2 sc in last sc: 5 sc.
Row 4: Ch 1, turn; 3 sc in first sc, sc in next 3 sc, 3 sc in last sc: 9 sc.
Row 5: Turn; slip st in first 3 sc, ch 1, sc in same st and in next 4 sc, leave remaining 2 sc unworked: 5 sc.
Row 6: Ch 1, turn; 2 sc in first sc, sc in next 3 sc, 2 sc in last sc: 7 sc.
Row 7: Ch 1, turn; 3 sc in first sc, sc in next 5 sc, 3 sc in last sc: 11 sc.
To **decrease**, pull up a loop in next 2 sc, YO and draw through all 3 loops on hook (**counts as one sc**).
To **double decrease**, pull up a loop in next 3 sc, YO and draw through all 4 loops on hook (**counts as one sc**).
Row 8: Turn; slip st in first 2 sc, ch 1, decrease, double decrease, decrease, leave remaining 2 sc unworked: 3 sc.
Row 9: Ch 1, turn; 2 sc in first sc, sc in next sc, 2 sc in last sc: 5 sc.
Row 10: Ch 1, turn; 3 sc in first sc, sc in next 3 sc, 3 sc in last sc: 9 sc.
Row 11: Turn; slip st in first 2 sc, ch 1, decrease, sc in next sc, decrease, leave remaining 2 sc unworked: 3 sc.
Row 12: Ch 1, turn; double decrease: 1 sc.
Row 13: Ch 1, turn; 3 sc in first sc.
Rows 14-288: Repeat Rows 2-13, 22 times; then repeat Rows 2-12 once **more**: 24 Leaves.
Finish off.

BORDER
Rnd 1: With **right** side facing, join Tan with slip st in last sc; ch 6, (tr in same st, ch 2) 5 times, † working in end of rows and at each point along edges of Leaves, sc in first point, ch 2, (sc in next point, ch 2) twice, ★ tr between Leaves, ch 2, (sc in next point, ch 2) 3 times; repeat from ★ across †; (tr, ch 2) 6 times in free loop of beginning ch (*Fig. 31b, page 124*), repeat from † to † once; join with slip st to fourth ch of beginning ch-6: 202 ch-2 sps.
Rnd 2: Slip st in first ch-2 sp, ch 1, (sc, ch 3, sc) in same sp and in each ch-2 sp around; join with slip st to first sc.
Rnd 3: Slip st in first ch-3 sp, ch 5, dc in same sp, (dc, ch 2, dc) in next ch-3 sp, (dc, ch 2, 2 dc, ch 2, dc) in next ch-3 sp, (dc, ch 2, dc) in next 99 ch-3 sps, place marker around last ch-2 sp worked for Rnd 4 placement, (dc, ch 2, dc) in next ch-2 sp, (dc, ch 2, 2 dc, ch 2, dc) in next ch-3 sp, (dc, ch 2, dc) in each ch-3 sp across; join with slip st to third ch of beginning ch-5, finish off: 204 ch-2 sps.
Rnd 4: With **right** side facing, join Red with slip st in marked ch-2 sp; (ch 1, sc, ch 3, sc) in same sp and in next 6 ch-2 sps, place marker around last ch-3 sp worked for joining placement, (ch 1, sc, ch 3, sc) in next 95 ch-2 sps, place marker around last ch-3 sp worked for joining placement, (ch 1, sc, ch 3, sc) in each ch-2 sp around; join with slip st to first sc, finish off.

REMAINING 10 STRIPS
Work same as First Strip through Rnd 3 of Border.
Rnd 4 (Joining rnd): With **right** side facing, join Red with slip st in marked ch-2 sp; (ch 1, sc, ch 3, sc) in same sp and in next 6 ch-2 sps, place marker around last ch-3 sp worked for joining placement, (ch 1, sc, ch 3, sc) in next 95 ch-2 sps, place marker around last ch-3 sp worked for joining placement, (ch 1, sc, ch 3, sc) in next 6 ch-2 sps, ch 1, sc in next ch-2 sp, ch 1, holding Strips with **wrong** sides together and bottom edges at the same end, slip st in first marked ch-3 sp on **previous Strip** (*Fig. 28, page 122*), ch 1, sc in same ch-2 sp on **new Strip**, ch 1, ★ sc in next ch-2 sp, ch 1, slip st in next ch-3 sp on **previous Strip**, ch 1, sc in same ch-2 sp on **new Strip**, ch 1; repeat from ★ across; join with slip st to first sc, finish off.

Using two strands of Red, add French-knot holly berries above and below each Leaf on Center of each Strip.

LITTLE GIRL'S FANCY

Sure to tickle a little girl's fancy, this afghan features rows of pink popcorn "posies" blooming against a yellow background of single crochets. Each strip is finished with a blue and white border and a pink picot edging.

Finished Size: 47" x 62"

MATERIALS
Worsted Weight Yarn:
Yellow - 20 ounces, (570 grams, 1,315 yards)
Green - 4 ounces, (110 grams, 265 yards)
Pink - 8 ounces, (230 grams, 530 yards)
Blue - 8 ounces, (230 grams, 530 yards)
White - 9 ounces, (260 grams, 590 yards)
Crochet hooks, sizes J (6.00 mm) **and** K (6.50 mm) **or** sizes needed for gauge

GAUGE: With larger size hook,
9 sc and 10 rows = 3"
Each Strip = 5¹/4" wide

FIRST STRIP
CENTER
With larger size hook and Yellow, ch 10 **loosely**.
Row 1: Sc in second ch from hook and in each ch across: 9 sc.
Rows 2 and 3: Ch 1, turn; sc in each sc across.
Row 4 (Right side): Ch 1, turn; sc in first 4 sc changing to Green in last sc *(Fig. 30a, page 124)*, sc in next sc changing to Yellow, sc in last 4 sc.
Note: Loop a short piece of yarn around any stitch to mark Row 4 as **right** side and bottom edge.
Row 5: Ch 1, turn; sc in first 3 sc changing to Green in last sc, sc in next 3 sc changing to Yellow in last sc, sc in last 3 sc.
Row 6: Ch 1, turn; sc in first 2 sc changing to Green in last sc, sc in next 2 sc changing to Yellow in last sc, sc in next sc changing to Green, sc in next 2 sc changing to Yellow in last sc, sc in last 2 sc.
Row 7: Ch 1, turn; sc in first 2 sc changing to Green in last sc, sc in next sc changing to Yellow, sc in next 3 sc changing to Green in last sc, sc in next sc changing to Yellow, sc in last 2 sc.
To work **Popcorn**, 5 dc in next sc, drop loop from hook, insert hook in first dc of 5-dc group, hook dropped loop and draw through *(Fig. 19, page 121)*.
Row 8: Ch 1, turn; sc in first 4 sc changing to Pink in last sc, work Popcorn, with Yellow ch 1 to close, sc in last 4 sc.
Rows 9-11: Ch 1, turn; sc in each st across: 9 sc.
Rows 12-192: Repeat Rows 4-11, 22 times; then repeat Rows 4-8 once more: 24 Flowers.
Rows 193-196: Ch 1, turn; sc in each st across.
Finish off.

BORDER
Rnd 1: With **right** side facing, using larger size hook, and working in end of rows, join Blue with sc in last row *(see Joining With Sc, page 124)*; (ch 1, skip next row, sc in next row) across to last row, ch 1, skip last row, working in free loops of beginning ch *(Fig. 31b, page 124)*, sc in ch at base of first st, ch 1, skip next 3 chs, (tr, ch 1) 7 times in next ch, skip next 3 chs, sc in last ch, (ch 1, skip next row, sc in next row) across, ch 1, skip first 4 sc on last row, (tr, ch 1) 7 times in next sc; join with slip st to first sc, finish off: 212 ch-1 sps.
Rnd 2: With **right** side facing and smaller size hook, join White with slip st in first ch-1 sp to left of last joining; ch 3, dc in same sp, 2 dc in each of next 97 ch-1 sps, (dc, ch 1, dc) in each of next 8 ch-1 sps, 2 dc in each of next 98 ch-1 sps, (dc, ch 1, dc) in each of next 8 ch-1 sps; join with slip st to top of beginning ch-3, finish off: 424 sts.
To work **Picot**, ch 4, slip st in third ch from hook, ch 1.
Rnd 3: With **right** side facing and smaller size hook, join Pink with slip st in sp **before** first st on last rnd *(Fig. 27, page 122)*; † (ch 3, skip next 2 dc, slip st in sp **before** next dc) 98 times, work Picot, (slip st in next ch-1 sp, work Picot) 8 times †, skip next dc, slip st in sp **before** next dc, repeat from † to † once; join with slip st to first slip st, finish off.

SECOND STRIP
Work same as First Strip through Rnd 2 of Border.
Rnd 3 (Joining rnd): With **right** side facing and smaller hook, join Pink with slip st in first ch-1 sp to right of last joining; ch 3, skip next dc, slip st in sp **before** next dc, (ch 3, skip next 2 dc, slip st in sp **before** next dc) 97 times, work Picot, skip next 2 dc, slip st in sp **before** next dc, (work Picot, slip st in next ch-1 sp) 8 times, ch 1, holding Strips with **wrong** sides together and bottom edges at the same end, slip st in corresponding ch-3 sp on **previous** Strip (last Strip made) *(Fig. 28, page 122)*, ch 1, slip st in sp **before** next dc on **new** Strip, ★ ch 1, slip st in next ch-3 sp on **previous** Strip, ch 1, skip next 2 dc on **new** Strip, slip st in sp **before** next dc; repeat from ★ 96 times **more**, work Picot, skip next 2 dc, slip st in sp **before** next dc, work Picot, (slip st in next ch-1 sp, work Picot) 7 times; join with slip st to first slip st, finish off.

THIRD STRIP

Work same as First Strip through Rnd 2 of Border.

Rnd 3 (Joining rnd): With **right** side facing and smaller size hook, join Pink with slip st in sp **before** first st on last rnd; (ch 3, skip next 2 dc, slip st in sp before next dc) 98 times, work Picot, (slip st in next ch-1 sp, work Picot) 8 times, skip next dc, slip st in sp **before** next dc, ch 1, holding Strips with **wrong** sides together and bottom edges at the same end, slip st in corresponding ch-3 sp on **previous** Strip (last Strip made), ch 1, skip next 2 dc on **new Strip**, slip st in sp **before** next dc, ★ ch 1, slip st in next ch-3 sp on **previous** Strip, ch 1, skip next 2 dc on **new Strip**, slip st in sp **before** next dc; repeat from ★ 96 times **more**, work Picot, (slip st in next ch-1 sp, work Picot) 8 times; join with slip st to first slip st, finish off.

REMAINING 6 STRIPS

Repeat Second and Third Strips, 3 times.

POPCORN BRAID

*Rounds of rust popcorn stitches add dimension to a
background of ecru double crochets on this classic afghan.
You'll be wrapped up in this winter warmer in no time!*

Finished Size: 49" x 68"

MATERIALS
Worsted Weight Yarn:
    Ecru - 34 ounces, (970 grams, 2,335 yards)
    Rust - 12 ounces, (340 grams, 825 yards)
    Lt Rust - 12 ounces, (340 grams, 825 yards)
    Dk Rust - 15 ounces, (430 grams, 1,030 yards)
Crochet hook, size H (5.00 mm) **or** size needed for gauge

GAUGE: 16 dc = 4" and 5 Popcorn rows = 4"
          Each Strip = 7" wide

STITCH GUIDE

BEGINNING RIGHT SIDE POPCORN
Ch 3, 4 dc in sp indicated, drop loop from hook, insert
hook from **front** to **back** in top of beginning ch-3, hook
dropped loop and draw through **(Fig. 19, page 121)**.
RIGHT SIDE POPCORN
5 Dc in sp indicated, drop loop from hook, insert hook
from **front** to **back** in first dc of 5-dc group, hook
dropped loop and draw through.
BEGINNING WRONG SIDE POPCORN
Ch 3, 4 dc in sp indicated, drop loop from hook, insert
hook from **back** to **front** in top of beginning ch-3, hook
dropped loop and draw through.
WRONG SIDE POPCORN
5 Dc in sp indicated, drop loop from hook, insert hook
from **back** to **front** in first dc of 5-dc group, hook
dropped loop and draw through.

STRIP (Make 7)
CENTER
With Rust, ch 5; join with slip st to form a ring.
Row 1 (Right side): Work (beginning right side Popcorn,
ch 2, right side Popcorn) in ring.
Note: Loop a short piece of yarn around any stitch to mark
Row 1 as **right** side and bottom edge.
Row 2: Turn; slip st in ch-2 sp, work (beginning wrong
side Popcorn, ch 2, wrong side Popcorn) in same sp.
Row 3: Turn; slip st in ch-2 sp, work (beginning right side
Popcorn, ch 2, right side Popcorn) in same sp.
Rows 4-73: Repeat Rows 2 and 3, 35 times.
Finish off.

BORDER
Rnd 1: With **right** side facing, join Ecru with slip st in
ch-2 sp on last row; ch 3 **(counts as first dc, now and
throughout)**, 9 dc in same sp, working along side of Center,
3 dc in ch-2 sp at base of each Popcorn across to beginning
ring, 10 dc in beginning ring, working along side of Center,
3 dc in ch-2 sp at top of each Popcorn across; join with
slip st to first dc: 72 3-dc groups **each** side.
Rnd 2: Ch 3, skip next dc, sc in sp **before** next dc
(Fig. 27, page 122), (ch 3, skip next 2 dc, sc in sp **before**
next dc) 4 times, (ch 3, sc in sp **before** next 3-dc group)
across, ch 3, skip next 3-dc group, sc in sp **before** next dc,
(ch 3, skip next 2 dc, sc in sp **before** next dc) 5 times,
(ch 3, sc in sp **before** next 3-dc group) across, ch 3; join with
slip st to base of beginning ch-3, finish off: 154 ch-3 sps.
Rnd 3: With **right** side facing, join Lt Rust with slip st in
first ch-3 sp to left of last joining; work beginning right side
Popcorn in same sp, (ch 2, work right side Popcorn) twice
in each of next 3 ch-3 sps, (ch 2, work right side Popcorn
in next ch-3 sp) 74 times, (ch 2, work right side Popcorn)
twice in each of next 3 ch-3 sps, ch 2, (work right side
Popcorn in next ch-3 sp, ch 2) across; join with slip st to
top of beginning right side Popcorn, finish off: 160 Popcorns.
Rnd 4: With **right** side facing, join Ecru with slip st in
first ch-2 sp to left of last joining; ch 3, 2 dc in same sp,
2 dc in next Popcorn, (2 dc in next ch-2 sp, 2 dc in next
Popcorn) 5 times, 3 dc in next 75 ch-2 sps, 2 dc in next
Popcorn, (2 dc in next ch-2 sp, 2 dc in next Popcorn) 5
times, 3 dc in each ch-2 sp across; join with slip st to first dc:
75 3-dc groups **each** side.
Rnd 5: Ch 3, skip next 3-dc group, sc in sp **before** next dc,
(ch 3, skip next 2 dc, sc in sp **before** next dc) 11 times,
(ch 3, sc in sp **before** next 3-dc group) 74 times, ch 3, skip
next 3-dc group, sc in sp **before** next dc, (ch 3, skip next
2 dc, sc in sp **before** next dc) 11 times, ch 3, (sc in sp
before next 3-dc group, ch 3) across; join with slip st to
base of beginning ch-3, finish off: 172 ch-3 sps.
Rnd 6: With **right** side facing, join Dk Rust with slip st in
ch-3 sp to left of last joining; work beginning right side
Popcorn in same sp, ch 2, (work right side Popcorn in next
ch-3 sp, ch 2) around; join with slip st to top of beginning
right side Popcorn, finish off: 172 Popcorns.

Rnd 7: With **right** side facing, join Ecru with slip st in ch-2 sp to left of last joining; ch 3, 2 dc in same sp, place marker around last dc made to mark joining placement, (4 dc in next ch-2 sp, 3 dc in next ch-2 sp) 5 times, place marker around first dc of 3-dc group just made to mark joining placement, 3 dc in next 76 ch-2 sps, place marker around last dc made to mark joining placement, (4 dc in next ch-2 sp, 3 dc in next ch-2 sp) 5 times, place marker around first dc of 3-dc group just made to mark joining placement, 3 dc in each ch-2 sp across; join with slip st to first dc, finish off.

ASSEMBLY

Place two Strips with **right** sides together and bottom edges at the same end. Working in **inside** loops only of **both** pieces, join Ecru with slip st in first marked dc; slip st in each st across to next marked dc, slip st in marked dc; finish off.

Join remaining Strips in same manner, always working in same direction.

EDGING

With **right** side facing, join Ecru with slip st in any st; ch 1, sc in same st and in each st and each joining around, increasing and decreasing as necessary to keep piece lying flat; join with slip st to first sc, finish off.

TASSELED RIBBONS

*Generous tassels accent the ends of this pretty afghan, which features
ribbons of mint green. To fashion the strips, a combination of front post and
back post stitches is bordered with treble, double, and half double crochets.*

Finished Size: 56" x 70"

MATERIALS
Worsted Weight Yarn:
  Off-White - 48 ounces, (1,360 grams, 3,040 yards)
  Green - 9 ounces, (260 grams, 570 yards)
Crochet hook, size I (5.50 mm) **or** size needed for gauge
Yarn needle

GAUGE: 12 dc and 6 rows = 4"
        Each Strip = 7" wide

STITCH GUIDE

FRONT POST DOUBLE CROCHET
  (abbreviated FPdc)
YO, insert hook from **front** to **back** around post of st
indicated, YO and pull up a loop (**Fig. 11, page 118**),
(YO and draw through 2 loops on hook) twice.

BACK POST DOUBLE CROCHET
  (abbreviated BPdc)
YO, insert hook from **back** to **front** around post of st
indicated, YO and pull up a loop (**Fig. 15, page 119**),
(YO and draw through 2 loops on hook) twice.

FRONT POST DOUBLE CROCHET DECREASE
  (abbreviated FPdc decrease) (uses next 2 sts)
★ YO, insert hook from **front** to **back** around post of
next st, YO and draw up a loop, YO and draw through
2 loops on hook; repeat from ★ once **more**, YO and draw
through all 3 loops on hook.

STRIP (Make 8)
CENTER
With Off-White, ch 6; join with slip st to form a ring.
Row 1: Ch 3 (**counts as first dc, now and throughout**),
(2 dc, ch 2, 3 dc) in ring: 6 dc.
Row 2 (Right side): Ch 3, turn; work FPdc around each of
next 2 dc, (dc, ch 2, dc) in next ch-2 sp, work FPdc around
each of next 2 dc, dc in last dc: 8 sts.
Note: Loop a short piece of yarn around any stitch to mark
Row 2 as **right** side and bottom edge.

Row 3: Ch 3, turn; work BPdc around each of next 2 FPdc,
(dc, ch 2, dc) in next ch-2 sp, skip next dc, work BPdc
around each of next 2 FPdc, dc in last dc.
Row 4: Ch 3, turn; work FPdc around each of next 2 BPdc,
(dc, ch 2, dc) in next ch-2 sp, skip next dc, work FPdc
around each of next 2 BPdc, dc in last dc.
Rows 5-85: Repeat Rows 3 and 4, 40 times; then repeat
Row 3 once **more**.
Row 86: Ch 3, turn; work FPdc decrease, (dc, ch 2, dc) in
next ch-2 sp, skip next dc, work FPdc decrease, dc in last
dc; do **not** finish off: 6 sts.

BORDER
Rnd 1: Ch 4 (**counts as first tr, now and throughout**),
working in end of rows, tr in first row, 2 dc in next row and
in each row across to last row, tr in last row, place marker
around tr just made for Rnd 2 joining, tr in same row, 11 tr
in beginning ring; working in end of rows, 2 tr in next row,
2 dc in each row across to last row, 2 tr in last row, 11 tr in
next ch-2 sp; join with slip st to first tr, finish off: 366 sts.
Rnd 2: With **right** side facing, join Green with slip st in sp
before marked tr (**Fig. 27, page 122**); ch 3, dc in same sp,
dc in sp **before** next tr, place marker around last dc made for
Rnd 3 joining, dc in sp **before** next 13 tr, 2 dc in sp **before**
next 2-dc group and **before** each 2-dc group across to next tr,
2 dc in sp **before** next tr, dc in sp **before** next tr, place marker
around last dc made, dc in sp **before** next 13 tr, 2 dc in sp
before next 2-dc group and **before** each 2-dc group across;
join with slip st to first dc, finish off: 170 2-dc groups.
Rnd 3: With **right** side facing, join Off-White with slip st
in sp **before** first marked dc; ch 3, dc in same sp, 2 dc in sp
before each of next 14 dc, ch 1, (dc in sp **before** next 2-dc
group, ch 1) across to next marked dc, 2 dc in sp **before**
each of next 15 dc, ch 1, (dc in sp **before** next 2-dc group,
ch 1) across; join with slip st to first dc: 30 2-dc groups.
Rnd 4: Slip st in sp **before** next dc; ch 2, hdc in sp **before**
next 5 dc, † place marker around last hdc made for joining
placement, hdc in sp **before** next 18 dc, place marker
around last hdc made for joining placement, hdc in sp
before next 5 dc, 2 hdc in each ch-1 sp across †, skip next
dc, hdc in sp **before** next 6 dc, repeat from † to † once; join
with slip st to top of beginning ch-2, finish off.

ASSEMBLY

Place two Strips with **wrong** sides together and bottom edges at the same end. Using Off-White and working through inside loops only, whipstitch Strips together, beginning in first marked hdc and ending in next marked hdc (**Fig. 33a, page 125**).

Join remaining Strips in same manner, always working in same direction.

EDGING

With **wrong** side facing, join yarn with slip st in any hdc on side of Strip; ch 3, dc in next hdc and in each hdc and joining around; join with slip st to first dc, finish off.

TASSELS

Make 16 tassels (**Figs. 35a & b, page 126**).
Attach one tassel to each end of each Strip.

TIMELESS TAPESTRY

*Cascading arches of double crochets in alternating shades
of rose and green create a soft, rippling tapestry of color on this
vintage wrap. Its timeless appeal will be enjoyed for years.*

Finished Size: 48" x 63"

MATERIALS
Worsted Weight Yarn:
Ecru - 16 ounces, (450 grams, 1,100 yards)
Green - 13 ounces, (370 grams, 895 yards)
Rose - 7 ounces, (200 grams, 480 yards)
Pink - 7 ounces, (200 grams, 480 yards)
Crochet hook, size J (6.00 mm) **or** size needed for gauge

GAUGE: Center = 2³/4" wide and 8 rows = 5"
Each Strip = 4³/4" wide

FIRST STRIP
To **decrease**, ★ YO, insert hook in **next** ch or st, YO and pull up a loop, YO and draw through 2 loops on hook; repeat from ★ once **more**, with color indicated YO and draw through all 3 loops on hook **(counts as one dc)**. With Pink, ch 10 **loosely**.

Row 1: Dc in third ch from hook and in next 2 chs, (dc, ch 1, dc) in next ch, dc in next 2 chs, decrease changing to Green **(Fig. 30a, page 124)**: 8 dc.

Row 2 (Right side): Ch 2, turn; dc in next 3 dc, (dc, ch 1, dc) in next ch-1 sp, dc in next 2 dc, decrease changing to Rose.

Note: Loop a short piece of yarn around any stitch to mark Row 2 as **right** side and bottom edge.

Row 3: Ch 2, turn; dc in next 3 dc, (dc, ch 1, dc) in next ch-1 sp, dc in next 2 dc, decrease changing to Green.

Row 4: Ch 2, turn; dc in next 3 dc, (dc, ch 1, dc) in next ch-1 sp, dc in next 2 dc, decrease changing to Pink.

Row 5: Ch 2, turn; dc in next 3 dc, (dc, ch 1, dc) in next ch-1 sp, dc in next 2 dc, decrease changing to Green.

Rows 6-96: Repeat **Rows 2-5**, 22 times; then repeat Rows 2-4 once **more**.

Row 97: Ch 2, turn; dc in next 3 dc, (dc, ch 1, dc) in next ch-1 sp, dc in next 2 dc, decrease, do **not** change color; finish off.

BORDER
Rnd 1: With **right** side facing, join Ecru with slip st in ch-1 sp on last row; ch 3, (dc, ch 1, 2 dc) in same sp, skip next 2 dc, (2 dc, ch 1, 2 dc) in next dc; working in end of rows, 2 hdc in first row, (2 dc in next row, 2 hdc in next row) across; working in free loops of beginning ch **(Fig. 31b, page 124)**, (2 dc, ch 1, 2 dc) in ch at base of first dc, ★ skip next 3 chs, (2 dc, ch 1, 2 dc) in next ch; repeat from ★ once **more**; working in end of rows, 2 hdc in first row, (2 dc in next row, 2 hdc in next row) across; working across last row, skip decrease, (2 dc, ch 1, 2 dc) in next dc; join with slip st to top of beginning ch-3.

Rnd 2: Slip st in next dc and in first ch-1 sp, ch 3, (2 dc, ch 3, 3 dc) in same sp, skip next 2 dc, sc in sp **before** next dc **(Fig. 27, page 122)**, skip next 2 dc, (2 dc, ch 3, 2 dc) in next ch-1 sp, skip next 2 dc, 2 hdc in next hdc, † skip next hdc, (sc, ch 3, sc) in next dc, skip next dc, 2 hdc in next hdc †, repeat from † to † across to within 3 sts of next ch-1 sp, skip next 3 sts, (2 dc, ch 3, 2 dc) in ch-1 sp, skip next 2 dc, sc in sp **before** next dc, (3 dc, ch 3, 3 dc) in next ch-1 sp, skip next 2 dc, sc in sp **before** next dc, (2 dc, ch 3, 2 dc) in next ch-1 sp, skip next 3 sts, 2 hdc in next hdc, ★ skip next dc, (sc, ch 3, sc) in next dc, skip next hdc, 2 hdc in next hdc; repeat from ★ across to within 2 dc of next ch-1 sp, skip next 2 dc, (2 dc, ch 3, 2 dc) in ch-1 sp, skip next 2 dc, sc in sp **before** next dc; join with slip st to top of beginning ch-3, finish off.

REMAINING 9 STRIPS
Work same as First Strip through Rnd 1 of Border.

Rnd 2 (Joining rnd): Slip st in next dc and in first ch-1 sp, ch 3, (2 dc, ch 3, 3 dc) in same sp, skip next 2 dc, sc in sp **before** next dc, (2 dc, ch 3, 2 dc) in next ch-1 sp, skip next 2 dc, 2 hdc in next hdc, † skip next hdc, (sc, ch 3, sc) in next dc, skip next dc, 2 hdc in next hdc †, repeat from † to † across to within 3 sts of next ch-1 sp, skip next 3 sts, (2 dc, ch 3, 2 dc) in next ch-1 sp, skip next 2 dc, sc in sp **before** next dc, (3 dc, ch 3, 3 dc) in next ch-1 sp, skip next 2 dc, sc in sp **before** next dc, (2 dc, ch 3, 2 dc) in next ch-1 sp, skip next 3 sts, 2 hdc in next hdc, skip next dc, sc in next dc, ch 1, holding Strips with **wrong** sides together and bottom edges at same end, slip st in corresponding ch-3 sp on **previous** Strip **(Fig. 28, page 122)**, ch 1, sc in same st on **new** Strip, ★ skip next hdc, 2 hdc in next hdc, skip next dc, sc in next dc, ch 1, slip st in next ch-3 sp on **previous** Strip, ch 1, sc in same st on **new** Strip; repeat from ★ across to within 4 sts of next ch-1 sp, skip next hdc, 2 hdc in next hdc, skip next 2 dc, (2 dc, ch 3, 2 dc) in next ch-1 sp, skip next 2 dc, sc in sp **before** next dc; join with slip st to top of beginning ch-3, finish off.

ARROWHEAD VALLEY

Featuring rows of flint-gray Indian "arrowheads,"
our throw has rugged style. The striking pattern is created
using a variety of basic stitches worked in rounds.

Finished Size: 47½" x 63½"

MATERIALS
Worsted Weight Yarn:
  Dk Gray - 24 ounces,
    (680 grams, 1,650 yards)
  Gray - 25 ounces,
    (710 grams, 1,715 yards)
Crochet hook, size G (4.00 mm) **or** size needed for gauge
Yarn needle

GAUGE: 16 sc = 4"
      Each Strip = 4¾" wide

STRIP (Make 10)
With Dk Gray, ch 218 **loosely**.
Rnd 1: Sc in second ch from hook and in next ch, hdc in next 2 chs, dc in next 2 chs, tr in next 2 chs, ch 3, slip st in same ch as last tr made, † sc in next 3 chs, hdc in next 2 chs, dc in next 2 chs, tr in next 2 chs, ch 3, slip st in same ch as last tr made †, repeat from † to † across to last 2 chs, sc in next ch, 3 sc in last ch, place marker around last sc made to mark **right** side and bottom edge; working in free loops of beginning ch *(Fig. 31b, page 124)*, sc in next ch, (slip st, ch 3, tr) in next ch, tr in next ch, dc in next 2 chs, hdc in next 2 chs, ★ sc in next 3 chs, (slip st, ch 3, tr) in next ch, tr in next ch, dc in next 2 chs, hdc in next 2 chs; repeat from ★ 22 times **more**, sc in next ch, 2 sc in same ch as first sc; join with slip st to first sc: 48 ch-3 sps.
Rnd 2: Ch 1, working in Back Loops Only *(Fig. 32, page 124)*, sc in first 8 sts, 3 sc in next ch, sc in next 2 chs, skip next slip st, slip st in next sc, † sc in next 8 sts, 3 sc in next ch, sc in next 2 chs, skip next slip st, slip st in next sc †, repeat from † to † 22 times **more**, sc in next sc, 3 sc in next sc, sc in next sc, slip st in next sc, skip next slip st, sc in next 2 chs, 3 sc in next ch, place marker in center sc of 3-sc group just made for Rnd 3 joining, sc in next 8 sts, ★ slip st in next sc, skip next slip st, sc in next 2 chs, 3 sc in next ch, sc in next 8 sts; repeat from ★ across to last sc, 3 sc in last sc; join with slip st to first sc, finish off: 632 sc.

Rnd 3: With **right** side facing and working in Back Loops Only, join Gray with slip st in marked sc; ch 1, sc in same st and in next 2 sc, hdc in next 2 sc, dc in next 2 sc, † tr in next 3 sc, skip next slip st and next 3 sc, sc in next 3 sc, hdc in next 2 sc, dc in next 2 sc †, repeat from † to † 22 times **more**, tr in next 2 sc, (tr, ch 3, sc) in next sc, sc in next 3 sc, (sc, ch 3, tr) in next sc, tr in next 2 sc, dc in next 2 sc, hdc in next 2 sc, sc in next 3 sc, ★ skip next 3 sc and next slip st, tr in next 3 sc, dc in next 2 sc, hdc in next 2 sc, sc in next 3 sc; repeat from ★ 22 times **more**, skip next 3 sc and next slip st, (tr, ch 3, sc) in next sc, sc in next 3 sc, (sc, ch 3, tr) in next sc, skip next slip st and last 3 sc; join with slip st to first sc: 492 sts and 4 ch-3 sps.
Rnd 4: Ch 1, sc in same st and in each st across to within one tr of next ch-3, † 3 sc in next tr, sc in next 3 chs and in next 5 sc, sc in next 3 chs, 3 sc in next tr †, sc in each st across to within one tr of next ch-3, repeat from † to † once; join with slip st to first sc: 512 sc.
Rnd 5: Ch 3 **(counts as first dc)**, ★ dc in next sc and in each sc across to center sc of next corner 3-sc group, 3 dc in center sc; repeat from ★ 3 times **more**, dc in last sc; join with slip st to first dc, finish off: 520 dc.
Rnd 6: With **right** side facing, join Dk Gray with slip st in center dc of any corner 3-dc group; ch 1, 3 sc in same dc, ★ sc in each dc across to center dc of next corner 3-dc group, 3 sc in center dc; repeat from ★ 2 times **more**, sc in each dc across; join with slip st to first sc, finish off: 528 sc.

ASSEMBLY

Place two Strips with **wrong** sides together and bottom edges at the same end. Using Dk Gray and working through inside loops only, whipstitch Strips together, beginning in center sc of first corner and ending in center sc of next corner *(Fig. 33a, page 125)*.

Join remaining Strips in same manner, always working in same direction.

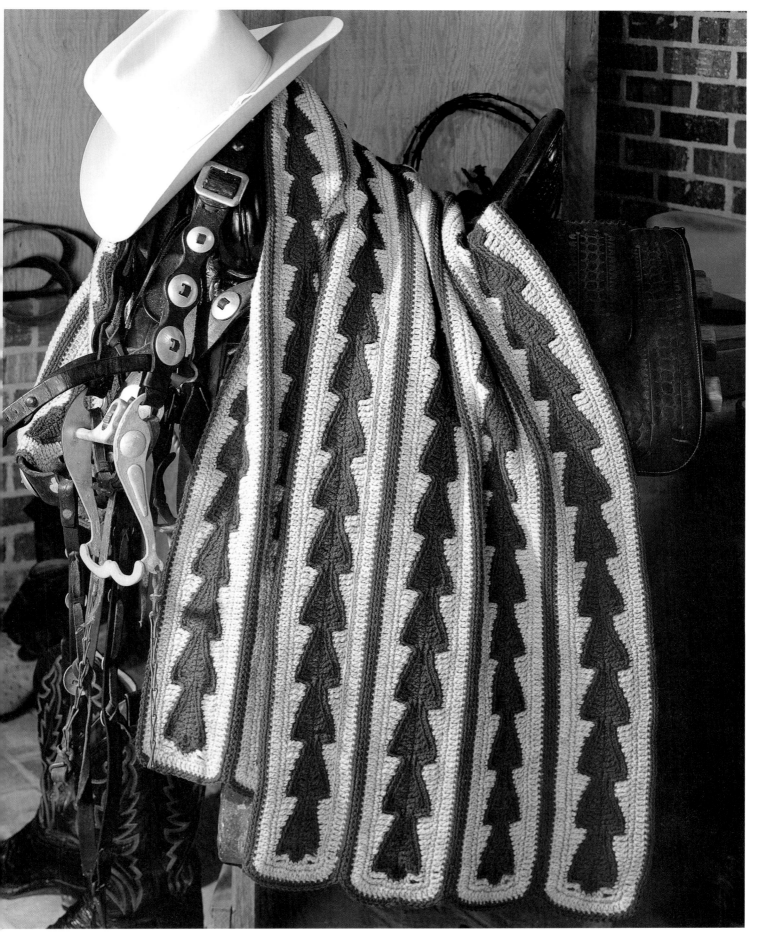

CHRISTMAS WREATHS

Our festive throw features merry wreaths accented with red yarn bows and French-knot "berries." A fanciful edging of ecru scallops finishes this Yuletide lovely.

Finished Size: 48" x 61"

MATERIALS
Worsted Weight Yarn:
  Green - 23 ounces, (655 grams, 1,510 yards)
  Ecru - 18 ounces, (510 grams, 1,185 yards)
  Red - 2 ounces, (60 grams, 130 yards)
Crochet hook, size H (5.00 mm) **or** size needed for gauge

GAUGE: Each Wreath = 2" wide and
    3 Wreaths = 5" long
    Each Strip = 4" wide

FIRST STRIP

To work **double treble crochet** *(abbreviated dtr)*, YO 3 times, insert hook in ch indicated, YO and pull up a loop, (YO and draw through 2 loops on hook) 4 times *(Figs. 8a & b, page 117)*.
Foundation Row: With Green, (ch 6, dtr in sixth ch from hook) 35 times: 35 loops.
Rnd 1 (Right side)**:** Working along dtr side of loops, slip st in first loop, ch 3 **(counts as first dc, now and throughout)**, 11 dc in same loop, slip st in same ch as dtr, (12 dc in next loop, slip st in same ch as dtr) 33 times, 24 dc in last loop; working along ch-6 side of loops, ★ slip st in same ch as corresponding slip st on previous side, 12 dc in next loop; repeat from ★ across; join with slip st to first dc, finish off: 35 Wreaths.
Note: Loop a short piece of yarn around any stitch to mark Rnd 1 as **right** side.
Rnd 2: With **right** side facing, join Ecru with slip st in fifth dc to left of last joining; ch 1, sc in same st, ch 3, sc in next dc, † ch 5, skip first 5 dc on next Wreath, sc in next dc, ch 3, sc in next dc †, repeat from † to † 33 times **more**, (ch 5, skip next 4 dc, sc in next dc, ch 3, sc in next dc) twice, repeat from † to † 34 times, ch 5, skip next 4 dc, sc in next dc, ch 3, sc in next dc, ch 5, skip last 4 dc; join with slip st to first sc.

Rnd 3: Slip st in first ch-3 sp, ch 3, dc in same sp, (ch 3, 2 dc in same sp) 3 times, slip st in next ch-5 sp, † 2 dc in next ch-3 sp, (ch 3, 2 dc in same sp) twice, slip st in next ch-5 sp †, repeat from † to † 32 times **more**, ★ 2 dc in next ch-3 sp, (ch 3, 2 dc in same sp) 3 times, slip st in next ch-5 sp; repeat from ★ 2 times **more**, repeat from † to † 33 times, [2 dc in next ch-3 sp, (ch 3, 2 dc in same sp) 3 times, slip st in next ch-5 sp] twice; join with slip st to first dc, finish off.

REMAINING 11 STRIPS

Work same as First Strip through Rnd 2.
Rnd 3 (Joining rnd)**:** Slip st in first ch-3 sp, ch 3, dc in same sp, (ch 3, 2 dc in same sp) 3 times, slip st in next ch-5 sp, † 2 dc in next ch-3 sp, (ch 3, 2 dc in same sp) twice, slip st in next ch-5 sp †, repeat from † to † 32 times **more**, [2 dc in next ch-3 sp, (ch 3, 2 dc in same sp) 3 times, slip st in next ch-5 sp] twice, 2 dc in next ch-3 sp, ch 3, 2 dc in same sp, ch 1, holding Strips with **wrong** sides together, slip st in corresponding ch-3 sp on **previous Strip** *(Fig. 28, page 122)*, ch 1, 2 dc in same sp on **new Strip**, ch 1, slip st in next ch-3 sp on **previous Strip**, ch 1, 2 dc in same sp on **new Strip**, ★ slip st in next ch-5 sp, 2 dc in next ch-3 sp, (ch 1, slip st in next ch-3 sp on **previous Strip**, ch 1, 2 dc in same sp on **new Strip**) twice; repeat from ★ 33 times **more**, ch 3, 2 dc in same sp, slip st in next ch-5 sp, 2 dc in next ch-3 sp, (ch 3, 2 dc in same sp) 3 times, slip st in next ch-5 sp; join with slip st to first dc, finish off.

FINISHING

Using photo as a guide for placement, add Red French Knots to every other Wreath.
Using a 7" length of Red, tie bow at base of each remaining Wreath; trim ends.

COUNTRY SPRINKLES

*Crocheted with color-sprinkled yarns, this country afghan
features circles that are formed as you work along each strip. The
burgundy centers are finished with natural and green borders.*

Finished Size: 48" x 65"

MATERIALS

Worsted Weight Yarn:
  Burgundy - 12¹/₂ ounces, (360 grams, 825 yards)
  Green - 8¹/₂ ounces, (240 grams, 560 yards)
  Natural - 27 ounces, (770 grams, 1,775 yards)
Crochet hook, size H (5.00 mm) **or** size needed for gauge
Yarn needle

GAUGE: Each Circle = 1³/₄" wide and
        2 Circles = 3¹/₂" long
        Each Strip = 4" wide

STITCH GUIDE

SC DECREASE
Pull up a loop in next dc, skip ch between Circles, pull up a loop in next dc, YO and draw through all 3 loops on hook.

DC DECREASE
YO, insert hook in next sc, YO and pull up a loop, YO and draw through 2 loops on hook, YO, skip next sc decrease, insert hook in next sc, YO and pull up a loop, YO and draw though 2 loops on hook, YO and draw through all 3 loops on hook.

TR DECREASE
† YO twice, working in **front** of sts on Rnd 2, insert hook in ch-1 sp **below** next ch, YO and pull up a loop, (YO and draw through 2 loops on hook) twice †, insert hook in next dc decrease and pull up a loop, repeat from † to † once, YO and draw through all 4 loops on hook.

STRIP (Make 12)

Foundation Circles: With Burgundy, ch 4, 15 dc in fourth ch from hook **(3 skipped chs count as first dc, now and throughout)**, loop a short piece of yarn around last dc made to mark **right** side, slip st in first dc, ★ ch 8, being careful not to twist ch, 7 dc in fourth ch from hook, skip first ch from previous Circle, and slip st in next ch **(counts as one dc)**, 7 dc in same ch as last 7 dc; join with slip st to first dc, mark **right** side of Circle; repeat from ★ 31 times **more**; finish off: 33 Circles.

Rnd 1: With **right** side facing, join Natural with sc in sixth dc to right of last joining **(see Joining With Sc, page 124)**; ch 1, (sc in next dc, ch 1) 12 times, sc decrease, ch 1, † (sc in next dc, ch 1) 5 times, sc decrease, ch 1 †, repeat from † to † 30 times **more**, (sc in next dc, ch 1) 13 times, sc decrease, ch 1, repeat from † to † 31 times; join with slip st to first sc, finish off.

Rnd 2: With **right** side facing, join Green with slip st in first sc to left of last joining; ch 4 **(counts as first dc plus ch 1)**, (dc in next sc, ch 1) 10 times, dc decrease, ch 1, † (dc in next sc, ch 1) 3 times, dc decrease, ch 1 †, repeat from † to † 30 times **more**, (dc in next sc, ch 1) 11 times, dc decrease, ch 1, repeat from † to † 31 times; join with slip st to first dc, finish off.

Rnd 3: With **right** side facing, join Natural with sc in same st as last joining; † (working **behind** next ch-1, tr in ch-1 sp on rnd **below**, sc in next dc) 10 times, tr decrease, ★ sc in next dc, (working **behind** next ch-1, tr in ch-1 sp on rnd **below**, sc in next dc) twice, tr decrease; repeat from ★ 30 times **more** †, sc in next dc, repeat from † to † once; join with slip st to first sc.

Rnd 4: Ch 1, sc in same st, (ch 1, sc in next st) 5 times, † place marker around last sc made for joining placement, (ch 1, sc in next st) 10 times, place marker around last sc made for joining placement, ch 1, (sc in next st, ch 1) 5 times, sc in sp **before** next tr decrease **(Fig. 27, page 122)**, ch 1, sc in sp **before** next sc, ch 1, ★ skip next sc, (sc in next st, ch 1) 4 times, sc in sp **before** next tr decrease, ch 1, sc in sp **before** next sc, ch 1; repeat from ★ 30 times **more** †, (ch 1, sc in next st) 6 times, repeat from † to † once; join with slip st to first sc, finish off.

ASSEMBLY

Place two Strips with **right** sides together. Working through **both** loops of **both** pieces, join Natural with slip st in first marked st; (ch 1, slip st in next sc) 5 times, ch 1, skip next ch-1 sp and next sc, slip st in next ch-1 sp, ★ ch 1, skip next sc and next ch-1 sp, (slip st in next sc, ch 1) 4 times, ch 1, skip next ch-1 sp and next sc, slip st in next ch-1 sp; repeat from ★ 30 times **more**, ch 1, skip next sc and next ch-1 sp, slip st in next sc, (ch 1, slip st in next sc) 5 times; finish off.

Join remaining Strips in same manner, always working in same direction.

BASKETWEAVE BEAUTY

*Alternating rows of cluster stitches in blue and
taupe are edged with double and treble crochets to create
a basketweave look on this old-fashioned beauty.*

Finished Size: 53" x 74"

MATERIALS
Worsted Weight Yarn:
Taupe - 25 ounces, (710 grams, 1,645 yards)
Blue - 24 ounces, (680 grams, 1,580 yards)
Crochet hook, size J (6.00 mm) **or** size needed for gauge
Yarn needle

GAUGE: 16 dc and 8 rows = 4"
Each Strip = 3" wide

STRIP A (Make 9)
CENTER
To work **Cluster**, ★ YO, insert hook in st indicated, YO
and pull up a loop, YO and draw through 2 loops on hook;
repeat from ★ 2 times **more**, YO and draw through all 4
loops on hook *(Figs. 17a & b, page 120)*.
With Taupe, ch 199 **loosely**.
Foundation Row (Right side)**:** Work Cluster in fourth ch
from hook, (ch 1, skip next ch, work Cluster in next ch)
across to last ch, dc in last ch; finish off: 98 Clusters.
Note: Loop a short piece of yarn around first Cluster
made to mark bottom edge and to mark Foundation Row
as **right** side.

BORDER
FIRST SIDE
With **right** side facing, join Blue with slip st in top of
beginning ch; ch 3 **(counts as first dc, now and
throughout)**, 2 dc in first Cluster, (ch 1, skip next ch,
2 dc in next Cluster) across to last dc, dc in last dc;
finish off: 198 dc.
SECOND SIDE
With **right** side facing and working in free loops of
beginning ch *(Fig. 31b, page 124)*, join Blue with slip st
in first ch; ch 3, 2 dc in next ch (at base of Cluster),
(ch 1, skip next ch, 2 dc in next ch) 97 times, dc in next
ch; finish off: 198 dc.

EDGING
To work **double treble crochet (abbreviated dtr)**, YO 3
times, insert hook in sp indicated, YO and pull up a loop,
(YO and draw through 2 loops on hook) 4 times
(Figs. 8a & b, page 117).
With **right** side facing and bottom edge at right, join Taupe
with slip st in second dc; ch 3, † place marker around dc
just made for joining placement, dc in next dc, ★ working
around next ch, tr in skipped ch on Foundation Row
(between Clusters), dc in next 2 dc; repeat from ★ across
to last dc, place marker around dc just made for joining
placement, leave last dc unworked; working in end of rows,
3 dc in first row, (2 tr, dtr, 2 tr) in next row, 3 dc in next
row †, skip first dc, dc in next dc, repeat from † to † once,
skip last dc; join with slip st to first dc, finish off.

STRIP B (Make 8)
Work same as Strip A, reversing colors.

ASSEMBLY
Note: Lay out Strips beginning with Strip A and
alternating Strips A and B throughout.

Place two Strips with **wrong** sides together and bottom
edges at the same end. Using Taupe and working through
inside loops only, whipstitch Strips together, beginning in
first marked dc and ending in next marked dc *(Fig. 33a,
page 125)*.

Join remaining Strips in same manner, always working in
same direction.

ALL-AROUND WRAP

Our all-around wrap will make a bright and cheerful addition to the bedroom. Foundation rows of white double crochets are accented with dark blue single crochets and light blue trebles on this simple afghan.

Finished Size: 45" x 61"

MATERIALS
Worsted Weight Yarn:
   White - 8 ounces, (230 grams, 525 yards)
   Dk Blue - 16 ounces, (450 grams, 1,045 yards)
   Lt Blue - 20 ounces, (570 grams, 1,305 yards)
Crochet hook, size G (4.00 mm) **or** size needed for gauge
Yarn needle

GAUGE: 16 dc = 4"
        Each Strip = 3" wide

STRIP (Make 15)
With White, ch 234 **loosely**.

Foundation Row: Dc in fourth ch from hook and in each ch across; finish off: 232 sts.

Note: Loop a short piece of yarn around any stitch to mark Foundation Row as **right** side.

Rnd 1: With **right** side facing, join Dk Blue with slip st around last dc made; ch 1, 3 sc in same sp; working in free loops of beginning ch **(Fig. 31b, page 124)**, sc in first 232 chs, 3 sc in end of row, sc in top of beginning ch and in each dc across; join with slip st to first sc: 470 sc.

Rnd 2: Ch 3 **(counts as first dc, now and throughout)**, dc in same st, † 3 dc in next sc, (2 dc in next sc, dc in next sc) twice, (ch 2, skip next 2 sc, dc in next 2 sc) 56 times †, ch 2, skip next 2 sc, (dc in next sc, 2 dc in next sc) twice, repeat from † to † once, ch 2, skip next 2 sc, dc in next sc, 2 dc in next sc, dc in next sc; join with slip st to top of first dc, finish off: 114 ch-2 sps.

Rnd 3: With **right** side facing, join Lt Blue with slip st in same st as last joining; ch 3, † working **around** next dc, 2 tr in sc **below** dc, (2 dc in next dc, 2 tr in sc **below** next dc) twice, dc in next 3 dc, place marker around last dc made for joining placement, (dc in next 2 dc, working **around** ch-2, tr in next 2 sc on rnd **below**) 57 times, dc in next 3 dc, place marker around last dc made for joining placement †, dc in next 2 dc, repeat from † to † once, dc in last dc; join with slip st to first dc, finish off.

ASSEMBLY
Place two Strips with **wrong** sides together. Using Lt Blue and working through both loops, whipstitch Strips together, beginning in first marked dc and ending in next marked dc **(Fig. 33b, page 125)**.

Join remaining Strips in same manner, always working in same direction.

GEMSTONE CABLES

Treat yourself like royalty with our jewel-tone wrap!
Treble stitches are worked behind more trebles to create
eye-catching cables on this gem of an afghan.

Finished Size: 48" x 64¹/2"

MATERIALS

Worsted Weight Yarn:
    Black - 12 ounces, (340 grams, 825 yards)
    Lt Teal - 12 ounces, (340 grams, 825 yards)
    Teal - 11 ounces, (310 grams, 755 yards)
    Purple - 11 ounces, (310 grams, 755 yards)
Crochet hook, size H (5.00 mm) **or** size needed for gauge
Yarn needle

GAUGE: Center = 3¹/4" wide and 8 rows = 3³/4"
        Each Strip = 4¹/4" wide

STRIP (Make 11)
CENTER

With Lt Teal, ch 14 **loosely**.

Row 1: Dc in fourth ch from hook and in next ch, ch 1, skip next 3 chs, tr in next 2 chs, working **behind** 2 tr just made, tr in second skipped ch and in next skipped ch, ch 1, skip next ch, dc in last 3 chs: 10 sts and 2 ch-1 sps.

Row 2 (Right side)**:** Ch 1, turn; sc in each st and in each ch-1 sp across changing to Purple in last sc **(Fig. 30a, page 124)**: 12 sc.

Note: Loop a short piece of yarn around any stitch to mark Row 2 as **right** side and bottom edge.

Row 3: Ch 3, turn; dc in next 2 sc, ch 1, skip next 3 sc, tr in next 2 sc, working **behind** 2 tr just made, tr in second skipped sc and in next skipped sc, ch 1, skip next sc, dc in last 3 sc: 10 sts and 2 ch-1 sps.

Row 4: Ch 1, turn; sc in each st and in each ch-1 sp across changing to Teal in last sc: 12 sc.

Rows 5 and 6: Repeat Rows 3 and 4 changing to Lt Teal in last sc on Row 6.

Rows 7 and 8: Repeat Rows 3 and 4 changing to Purple in last sc on Row 6.

Rows 9-133: Repeat Rows 3-8, 20 times; then repeat Rows 3-7 once **more**.

Finish off.

BORDER

With **right** side facing and working in end of rows, join Black with slip st in last row; ch 3, (dc, ch 1, 2 dc) in same sp, † (skip next sc row, 2 dc **around** first 2 dc on next row) across to last 2 rows, skip next sc row, (2 dc, ch 1, 2 dc) in last row †; working across beginning ch, dc in next ch-1 sp, skip next 2 tr, (3 dc, ch 2, 3 dc) in sp **before** next tr *(Fig. 27, page 122)*, dc in next ch-1 sp; working in end of rows, (2 dc, ch 1, 2 dc) in first row, repeat from † to † once; working across last row, dc in next ch-1 sp, skip next 2 tr, (3 dc, ch 2, 3 dc) in sp **before** next tr, dc in next ch-1 sp; join with slip st to first dc, finish off.

ASSEMBLY

Place two Strips with **right** sides together and bottom edges at the same end. Working through **both** loops of **both** pieces, join Black with slip st in first corner ch-1 sp, slip st in each dc across to next corner ch-1 sp, slip st in ch-1 sp; finish off.

Join remaining Strips in same manner, always working in same direction.

EDGING

With **right** side facing, join Black with slip st in ch-1 sp at top right corner; ch 3, (dc, ch 1, 2 dc) in same sp, † skip next 2 dc, dc in next 3 dc, skip next dc, (3 dc, ch 2, 3 dc) in next ch-2 sp, skip next dc, dc in next 3 dc, ★ skip next 2 dc, (2 dc, ch 1, 2 dc) in next joining, skip next 2 dc, dc in next 3 dc, skip next dc, (3 dc, ch 2, 3 dc) in next ch-2 sp, skip next dc, dc in next 3 dc; repeat from ★ 9 times **more**, skip next 2 dc, (2 dc, ch 1, 2 dc) in next ch-1 sp, skip next dc, dc in next dc and in each dc across to within one dc of next ch-1 sp, skip next dc †, (2 dc, ch 1, 2 dc) in ch-1 sp, repeat from † to † once; join with slip st to first dc, finish off.

BLUEBERRY COBBLER

*This afghan will be Grandpa's first pick! Deliciously delightful,
our old-fashioned wrap is topped off with popcorn "blueberries"
and double crochet "scoops" of vanilla ice cream.*

Finished Size: 45" x 61"

MATERIALS

Worsted Weight Yarn:

Tan - 17 ounces, (480 grams, 1,045 yards)

Lt Tan - 11 ounces, (310 grams, 675 yards)

Blue - 10 ounces, (280 grams, 615 yards)

Crochet hook, size I (5.50 mm) **or** size needed for gauge

GAUGE: Rnds 1 and 2 = 2¹/₂" wide and
2 repeats = 3³/₄" long
Each Strip = 4¹/₂" wide

FIRST STRIP

Foundation Row: With Lt Tan, (ch 4, dc in fourth ch from hook) 61 times: 61 loops.

Rnd 1 (Right side)**:** Ch 1, working along dc side of loops, (sc, 5 dc) in first loop, sc in next loop, (5 dc in next loop, sc in next loop) across to last loop, (5 dc, sc, 5 dc) in last loop, working along ch-4 side of loops, sc in next loop, (5 dc in next loop, sc in next loop) across, 5 dc in same loop as first sc; with Blue, join with slip st to first sc *(Fig. 30b, page 124)*: 62 5-dc groups.

Note: Loop a short piece of yarn around any stitch to mark Row 1 as **right** side.

To work **Popcorn,** 5 dc in st indicated, drop loop from hook, insert hook in first dc of 5-dc group, hook dropped loop and draw through *(Fig. 19, page 121)*.

Rnd 2: Ch 3, 4 dc in same st, drop loop from hook, insert hook in top of beginning ch, hook dropped loop and draw through, ch 4, work Popcorn in same st, † ch 3, skip next 2 dc, sc in next dc, (ch 2, skip next 2 dc, work Popcorn in next sc, ch 2, skip next 2 dc, sc in next dc) 30 times, ch 3, skip next 2 dc †, work (Popcorn, ch 4, Popcorn) in next sc, repeat from † to † once; with Tan, join with slip st to top of first st: 64 Popcorns.

Rnd 3: Ch 1, sc in same st, † 5 sc in next ch-4 sp, sc in next st, 4 sc in next ch-3 sp, sc in next st, (2 sc in next ch-2 sp, sc in next st) 60 times, 4 sc in next ch-3 sp †, sc in next st, repeat from † to † once; join with slip st to first sc: 392 sc.

Rnd 4: Ch 1, (sc, ch 2, dc) in same st, skip next sc, ★ (sc, ch 2, dc) in next sc, skip next sc; repeat from ★ around; join with slip st to first sc: 196 ch-2 sps.

Rnd 5: Slip st in first ch-2 sp, ch 1, sc in same sp, (ch 3, sc in next ch-2 sp) 3 times, (ch 2, sc in next ch-2 sp) 3 times, place marker around last ch-2 sp made for joining placement, (ch 2, sc in next ch-2 sp) 90 times, place marker around last ch-2 sp made for joining placement, (ch 2, sc in next ch-2 sp) twice, (ch 3, sc in next ch-2 sp) 3 times, ch 2, (sc in next ch-2 sp, ch 2) across; join with slip st to first sc, finish off.

REMAINING 9 STRIPS

Work same as First Strip through Rnd 4.

Rnd 5 (Joining rnd)**:** Slip st in first ch-2 sp, ch 1, sc in same sp, (ch 3, sc in next ch-2 sp) 3 times, (ch 2, sc in next ch-2 sp) 3 times, place marker around last ch-2 sp made for joining placement, (ch 2, sc in next ch-2 sp) 90 times, place marker around last ch-2 sp made for joining placement, (ch 2, sc in next ch-2 sp) twice, (ch 3, sc in next ch-2 sp) 3 times, (ch 2, sc in next ch-2 sp) twice, ch 1, holding Strips with **wrong** sides together, slip st in first marked sp on **previous Strip** *(Fig. 28, page 122)*, ch 1, sc in next ch-2 sp on **new Strip**, ★ ch 1, slip st in next ch-2 sp on **previous Strip**, ch 1, sc in next ch-2 sp on **new Strip**; repeat from ★ 89 times **more**, ch 2, sc in next ch-2 sp, ch 2; join with slip st to first sc, finish off.

RUBIES & PEARLS

Strung with double crochet "pearls" and treble crochet "rubies,"
this precious cover-up lends feminine appeal wherever it's displayed.
The afghan will undoubtedly become a treasured keepsake!

Finished Size: 49" x 63"

MATERIALS
Worsted Weight Yarn:
  Natural - 19 ounces, (540 grams, 1,305 yards)
  Rose - 11 ounces, (310 grams, 755 yards)
  Dk Rose - 23 ounces, (650 grams, 1,580 yards)
Crochet hook, size I (5.50 mm) **or** size needed for gauge
Yarn needle

GAUGE: Each Circle = 1⅞" wide
Each Strip = 3¾" wide

STRIP (Make 13)
Foundation Circles: With Dk Rose, ch 4, dc in top 2 loops of fourth ch from hook *(Fig. 2b, page 116)* **(3 skipped chs count as first dc, now and throughout)**, ch 3, (3 dc in same ch, ch 3) 3 times, dc in same ch, loop a short piece of yarn around last dc made to mark **right** side, slip st in first dc, ★ ch 12, dc in top 2 loops of fourth ch from hook, ch 3, 3 dc in same ch, ch 3, dc in same ch, slip st in sixth ch from previous Circle **(counts as one dc)**, dc in same ch as last dc, ch 3, 3 dc in same ch, ch 3, dc in same ch, mark last dc made as **right** side, slip st in first dc on new Circle; repeat from ★ 19 times **more**; finish off: 21 Circles.

Rnd 1: With **right** side facing, join Rose with slip st in second ch-3 sp to **right** of last slip st; ch 1, (sc in same sp, sc in next 3 dc and in next ch-3 sp, working in **front** of same ch-3, tr in ch **below** ch-3) 3 times, 3 dc around ch between Circles, being careful not to twist Circles and working in **front** of next ch-3 on next Circle, tr in ch **below** same ch-3, † sc in same ch-3 sp, sc in next 3 dc and in next ch-3 sp, working in **front** of same ch-3, tr in ch **below** ch-3, 3 dc around ch between Circles, working in **front** of next ch-3 on next Circle, tr in ch **below** same ch-3 †, repeat from † to † 18 times **more**, (sc in same sp, sc in next 3 dc and in next ch-3 sp, working in **front** of same ch-3, tr in ch **below** same sp) 3 times, working around ch between Circles, dc **between** lower loops of next 3 dc *(Fig. 22, page 121)*, working in **front** of next ch-3 on next Circle, tr in ch **below** same ch-3, ★ sc in same ch-3 sp, sc in next 3 dc and in next ch-3 sp, working in **front** of same ch-3, tr in ch **below** ch-3, working over ch between Circles, dc **between** lower loops of next 3 dc, working in **front** of next ch-3 on next Circle, tr in ch **below** same ch-3; repeat from ★ across; join with slip st to first sc, finish off.

To **decrease**, YO twice, working in **front** of previous rnd and to **right** of next tr, insert hook in sp **behind** tr, YO and pull up a loop, (YO and draw through 2 loops on hook) twice, YO twice, working in **front** of previous rnd and to **left** of same tr, insert hook in same ch-3 sp, YO and pull up a loop, (YO and draw through 2 loops on hook) twice, YO and draw through all 3 loops on hook.

Rnd 2: With **right** side facing, join Natural with slip st in same sc as last joining; ch 3 **(counts as first dc, now and throughout)**, dc in same st and in next sc, 2 dc in next sc, dc in next sc, 2 dc in next sc, decrease, [2 dc in next sc, (dc in next sc, 2 dc in next sc) twice, decrease] twice, skip next dc, sc in next dc, skip next dc, decrease, † 2 dc in next sc, (dc in next sc, 2 dc in next sc) twice, decrease, skip next dc, sc in next dc, skip next dc, decrease †, repeat from † to † 18 times **more**, [2 dc in next sc, (dc in next sc, 2 dc in next sc) twice, decrease] 3 times, skip next dc, sc in next dc, skip next dc, decrease, repeat from † to † across; join with slip st to first dc.

To work **Cluster**, † YO, insert hook in next st, YO and pull up a loop, YO and draw through 2 loops on hook †, YO twice, insert hook in next sc, YO and pull up a loop, (YO and draw through 2 loops on hook) twice, repeat from † to † once, YO and draw through all 4 loops on hook *(Figs. 17c & d, page 120)*.

Rnd 3: With **right** side facing, join Dk Rose with slip st in same st as last joining; ch 3, † hdc in next dc, (ch 1, sc in next st) 6 times, place marker around last ch-1 made for joining placement, (ch 1, sc in next st) 12 times, place marker around last ch-1 made for joining placement, (ch 1, sc in next st) 4 times, ch 1, hdc in next dc, dc in next dc, work Cluster, ★ dc in next dc, hdc in next dc, ch 1, (sc in next st, ch 1) 4 times, hdc in next dc, dc in next dc, work Cluster; repeat from ★ 18 times **more** †, dc in next dc, repeat from † to † once; join with slip st to first dc, finish off.

ASSEMBLY
Place two Strips with **wrong** sides together. Using Dk Rose and working through both loops, whipstitch Strips together, beginning in first marked ch and ending in next marked ch *(Fig. 33b, page 125)*.

Join remaining Strips in same manner, always working in same direction.

SPRING CARNIVAL

*Finished in a flash using basic crochet stitches, this
refreshing cover-up is the perfect project for quiet spring days.
Its classic style will make it a year-round favorite.*

Finished Size: 54" x 73"

MATERIALS
Worsted Weight Yarn:
Variegated - 15 ounces, (430 grams, 985 yards)
Ecru - 15¹/₂ ounces, (440 grams, 1,020 yards)
Blue - 17 ounces, (480 grams, 1,120 yards)
Crochet hook, size J (6.00 mm) **or** size needed for gauge
Yarn needle

GAUGE: 16 dc and 8 rows = 4"
Each Strip = 3¹/₂" wide

STRIP (Make 15)
CENTER
With Variegated, ch 6 **loosely**.
Row 1: Sc in second ch from hook and in each ch across:
5 sc.
Row 2 (Right side)**:** Ch 3 **(counts as first dc, now and
throughout)**, turn; skip next sc, 3 dc in next sc (center sc),
skip next sc, dc in last sc: 5 dc.
Note: Loop a short piece of yarn around any stitch to mark
Row 2 as **right** side and bottom edge.
Rows 3-116: Ch 3, turn; skip next dc, 3 dc in next dc
(center dc), skip next dc, dc in last dc.
Row 117: Ch 1, turn; sc in each dc across; finish off.

BORDER
With **right** side facing and working in end of rows, join
Ecru with slip st in Row 2; ch 3, dc in same row, (ch 1,
2 dc in next row) across to last row (sc row), ch 2, skip last
row and first sc, 2 dc in next sc, ch 2, skip next sc, 2 dc in
next sc, ch 2, skip last sc and first row (sc row); working in
end of rows, 2 dc in next row, (ch 1, 2 dc in next row)
across to last row (sc row), ch 2, skip last row; working in
free loops of beginning ch *(Fig. 31b, page 124)*, skip ch at
base of first sc, (2 dc in next ch, ch 2, skip next ch) twice;
join with slip st to first dc, finish off: 468 dc.

TRIM
FIRST SIDE
With **right** side facing, join Blue with slip st in same st as
joining; ch 3, dc in next dc, (ch 1, skip next ch-1 sp, dc in
next 2 dc) 114 times; finish off: 230 dc.
SECOND SIDE
With **right** side facing, skip next 4 dc and join Blue with
slip st in next dc; ch 3, dc in next dc, (ch 1, skip next
ch-1 sp, dc in next 2 dc) 114 times, leave remaining 4 dc
unworked; finish off: 230 dc.

ASSEMBLY
Place two Strips with **wrong** sides together and bottom edges
at the same end. Using Blue and working through inside loops
only, whipstitch Strips together, beginning in first dc of
Trim and ending in last dc of Trim *(Fig. 33a, page 125)*.

Join remaining Strips in same manner, always working in
same direction.

EDGING
With **right** side facing, join Blue with slip st in first dc at
bottom right corner; ch 2, dc in same st and in next dc,
† skip next ch-1 sp, (dc in next 2 dc, skip next ch-1 sp)
across to last 2 dc, dc in next dc, (dc, ch 2, slip st) in last dc,
3 dc in next ch-2 sp (on Border of first Strip), (2 dc in each
of next 2 dc, 3 dc in next ch-2 sp) twice, ★ slip st in joining,
3 dc in next ch-2 sp (on Border of next Strip), (2 dc in
each of next 2 dc, 3 dc in next ch-2 sp) twice; repeat from
★ across to corner †, (slip st, ch 2, dc) in first dc, dc in next
dc, repeat from † to † once; join with slip st to first slip st,
finish off.

MAJESTIC MILES

Treble stitches and front post trebles give this majestic afghan rich texture. An ideal companion for road trips, the handsome wrap is worked in an eye-pleasing combination of black and variegated yarns.

Finished Size: 47" x 63"

MATERIALS
Worsted Weight Yarn:
    Black - 16 ounces, (450 grams, 1,100 yards)
    Variegated - 38 ounces, (1,080 grams, 2,610 yards)
Crochet hook, size G (4.00 mm) **or** size needed for gauge
Yarn needle

GAUGE: Center = 1" wide and 8 rows = 4¹/₂"
             Each Strip = 5¹/₄" wide

STRIP (Make 9)
CENTER
With Black, ch 6; join with slip st to form a ring.
Row 1: Ch 1, 4 sc in ring.
Row 2 (Right side): Turn; skip first sc, slip st in next sc, ch 3 **(counts as first dc, now and throughout)**, dc in next 2 sc, working in **front** of 3 dc just made and inserting hook from **back** to **front**, tr in slip st at base of first dc: 4 sts.
Note: Loop a short piece of yarn around any stitch to mark Row 2 as **right** side and bottom edge.
Row 3: Ch 1, turn; sc in each st across.
Rows 4-101: Repeat Rows 2 and 3, 49 times.
Row 102: Ch 3, turn; skip first 3 sc, slip st in last sc; finish off.

BORDER
Rnd 1: With **right** side facing, join Variegated with slip st in ch-3 sp on last row; ch 3, 8 dc in same sp; working in end of rows, dc in next sc row, (3 dc in next row, dc in next sc row) across, 9 dc in beginning ring; working in end of rows, dc in first sc row, (3 dc in next row, dc in next sc row) across; join with slip st to first dc: 420 dc.
Rnd 2: Ch 1, 2 sc in same st, † tr in next dc, (2 sc in next dc, tr in next dc) 4 times, (sc in next dc, tr in next dc) across to next 9-dc group †, 2 sc in next dc, repeat from † to † once; join with slip st to first sc, finish off: 430 sts.

Rnd 3: With **right** side facing, join Black with slip st in same st as joining; ch 4 **(counts as first tr)**, tr in next sc, † (2 sc in next tr, tr in next 2 sc) 4 times, sc in next tr, (tr in next sc, sc in next tr) 100 times †, tr in next 2 sc, repeat from † to † once; join with slip st to first tr, finish off: 438 sts.
Rnd 4: With **right** side facing, join Variegated in same st as joining; ch 3, dc in next 3 sts, † 2 dc in each of next 2 tr, (dc in next 2 sc, 2 dc in each of next 2 tr) twice †, dc in next 209 sts, repeat from † to † once, dc in each st across; join with slip st to first dc: 450 dc.
To work **Front Post treble crochet** *(abbreviated FPtr)*, YO twice, insert hook from **front** to **back** around post of tr in row **below** next dc, YO and pull up a loop *(Fig. 12, page 118)*, (YO and draw through 2 loops on hook) 3 times. Do **not** skip st behind FPtr, unless otherwise instructed.
Rnd 5: Slip st in next 2 sts, ch 3, dc in next 2 dc, † work FPtr, dc in next 2 dc, work FPtr, (dc in next 4 dc, work FPtr, dc in next 2 dc, work FPtr) twice, dc in next 3 dc, work FPtr twice, skip 2 dc behind 2 FPtr just made, dc in next dc, (work FPtr, skip dc behind FPtr, dc in next dc) 100 times, work FPtr twice †, skip 2 dc behind 2 FPtr just made, dc in next 3 dc, repeat from † to † once working last 2 FPtr over beginning slip sts; join with slip st to first dc: 462 sts.
Rnd 6: Ch 1, sc in same st and in next 28 sts, place marker around last sc made for joining placement, sc in next 200 sts, place marker around last sc made for joining placement, sc in next 31 sts, place marker around last sc made for joining placement, sc in next 200 sts, place marker around last sc made for joining placement, sc in last 2 sts; join with slip st to first sc, finish off.

ASSEMBLY
Place two Strips with **wrong** sides together and bottom edges at the same end. Using Variegated and working through inside loops only, whipstitch Strips together, beginning in first marked sc and ending in next marked sc *(Fig. 33a, page 125)*.

Join remaining Strips in same manner, always working in same direction.

ROPES OF JADE

Resembling ropes of jade beads, this afghan is quite a beauty!
A foundation row of double crochets begins the lush blanket of green,
with front post double crochets creating a textured trim.

Finished Size: 52¹/₂ " x 72"

MATERIALS
Worsted Weight Yarn:
Lt Green - 30 ounces, (850 grams, 1,970 yards)
Green - 24 ounces, (680 grams, 1,575 yards)
Crochet hook, size G (4.00 mm) **or** size needed for gauge
Yarn needle

GAUGE: 16 dc and 8 rows = 4"
Each Strip = 3¹/₂" wide

STRIP (Make 15)
CENTER
With Green, ch 279 **loosely**.
Foundation Row (Right side)**:** Dc in fourth ch from hook
and in each ch across; finish off: 277 sts.
Note: Loop a short piece of yarn around last dc made
to mark bottom edge and to mark Foundation Row as
right side.

TRIM
FIRST SIDE
To work **Front Post double crochet** *(abbreviated FPdc),*
YO, insert hook from **front** to **back** around post of st
indicated, YO and pull up a loop *(Fig. 11, page 118)*,
(YO and draw through 2 loops on hook) twice.
Row 1: With **right** side facing, join Lt Green with slip st in
top of beginning ch; ch 3 **(counts as first dc, now and
throughout)**, skip next dc, 3 dc in next dc, ★ skip next dc,
work FPdc around next dc, skip dc behind FPdc **and** next
dc, 3 dc in next dc; repeat from ★ across to last 2 dc, skip
next dc, dc in last dc; finish off: 209 dc and 68 FPdc.
Row 2: With **right** side facing, join Green with slip st in
first dc; ch 3, skip next dc, dc in next dc, place marker
around last dc made for Border placement, 2 dc in same dc,
★ skip next dc, work FPdc around next FPdc, skip next dc,
3 dc in next dc; repeat from ★ across to last 2 dc, skip next
dc, dc in last dc; finish off.

TRIM
SECOND SIDE
Row 1: With **right** side facing and working in free loops
of beginning ch *(Fig. 31b, page 124)*, join Lt Green with
slip st in first ch; ch 3, skip next ch, 3 dc in next ch, ★ skip
next ch, work FPdc around next dc on Foundation Row,
skip ch behind FPdc **and** next ch, 3 dc in next ch; repeat
from ★ 67 times **more**, skip next ch, dc in next ch; finish off:
209 dc and 68 FPdc.
Row 2: With **right** side facing, join Green with slip st in
first dc; ch 3, skip next dc, 3 dc in next dc, ★ skip next dc,
work FPdc around next FPdc, skip next dc, 3 dc in next dc;
repeat from ★ across to last 2 dc, skip next dc, dc in last dc;
finish off.

BORDER
With **right** side facing and working in Back Loops Only
(Fig. 32, page 124), join Lt Green with slip st in marked
dc; ch 3, place marker around last dc made for joining
placement, † dc in next dc and in each st across to last dc,
leave last dc unworked, place marker around last dc made
for joining placement; working in end of rows, 3 dc in each
of first 2 rows, 5 tr in Foundation Row, 3 dc in each of next
2 rows †, skip first dc, dc in next dc, place marker around
last dc made for joining placement, repeat from † to † once;
join with slip st to first dc, finish off: 584 sts.

ASSEMBLY
Place two Strips with **wrong** sides together and bottom
edges at the same end. Using Lt Green and working
through inside loops only, whipstitch Strips together,
beginning in first marked dc and ending in next marked
dc *(Fig. 33a, page 125)*.

Join remaining Strips in same manner, always working in
same direction.

COZY COVER-UP

*Warm hues of red and beige give this cozy cover-up homey appeal.
Treble and post stitches create the simple pattern.*

Finished Size: 52" x 66"

MATERIALS
Worsted Weight Yarn:
    Red - 31 ounces, (880 grams, 1,950 yards)
    Beige - 27 ounces, (770 grams, 1,695 yards)
    Crochet hook, size I (5.50 mm) **or** size needed for gauge
    Yarn needle

GAUGE: Center = 1¼" wide and 8 rows = 4"
              Each Strip = 3¼" wide

STRIP (Make 16)
CENTER
With Beige, ch 7 **loosely**.
Row 1 (Right side): Dc in fourth ch from hook **(3 skipped chs count as first dc)**, ch 1, skip next ch, dc in last 2 chs: 4 dc.
Note: Loop a short piece of yarn around any stitch to mark Row 1 as **right** side and bottom edge.
Rows 2-127: Ch 3 **(counts as first dc, now and throughout)**, turn; dc in next dc, ch 1, dc in last 2 dc. Finish off.

BORDER
To work **Front Post treble crochet (*abbreviated FPtr*)**, YO twice, insert hook from **front** to **back** around post of st indicated, YO and pull up a loop **(Fig. 12, page 118)**, (YO and draw through 2 loops on hook) 3 times. Skip st behind FPtr.
Rnd 1: With **right** side facing, join Red with slip st in right end of last row; ch 3, 5 dc in same row; working across last row, † skip first dc, work FPtr around each of next 2 dc , skip last dc; working in end of rows, 6 dc in first row, working in **front** of first dc, tr around second dc on next row, (3 dc in next row, working in **front** of first dc, tr around second dc on next row) across to last row †, 6 dc in last row; working across first row, repeat from † to † once; join with slip st to first dc: 526 sts.

To work **Front Post half double crochet (*abbreviated FPhdc*)**, YO, insert hook from **front** to **back** around post of st indicated, YO and pull up a loop **(Fig. 10, page 118)**, YO and draw through all 3 loops on hook. Skip st behind FPhdc.
Rnd 2: Ch 1, working in Back Loops Only **(Fig. 32, page 124)**, sc in same st and in next 2 dc, † 2 sc in next dc, sc in next dc, 2 sc in next dc, work FPhdc around each of next 2 FPtr, 2 sc in next dc, sc in next dc, 2 sc in next dc, (sc in next 3 dc, work FPhdc around next tr) 63 times †, sc in next 3 dc, repeat from † to † once; join with slip st to Back Loop Only of first sc, finish off: 534 sts.
Rnd 3: With **right** side facing and working in Back Loops Only, join Beige with slip st in same st as joining; ch 1, sc in same st and in next 2 sc, † place marker around last sc made for joining placement, (sc in next st, 2 sc in next st) 5 times, sc in next 3 sc, place marker around last sc made for joining placement †, sc in next 254 sc, repeat from † to † once, sc in each sc across; join with slip st to **both** loops of first sc, finish off.

ASSEMBLY
Place two Strips with **wrong** sides together and bottom edges at the same end. Using Beige and working through inside loops only, whipstitch Strips together, beginning in first marked sc and ending in next marked sc **(Fig. 33a, page 125)**.

Join remaining Strips in same manner, always working in same direction.

SENTIMENTAL SHELLS

Sweet ruffled layers of double crochets make this sentimental afghan ideal for wrapping up in for an idyllic afternoon on the porch swing.

Finished Size: 45" x 65"

MATERIALS
Worsted Weight Yarn:
- Lt Purple - 16 ounces, (450 grams, 1,055 yards)
- Purple - 12 ounces, (340 grams, 790 yards)
- Dk Purple - 12 ounces, (340 grams, 790 yards)
- Black - 7 ounces, (200 grams, 460 yards)

Crochet hook, size H (5.00 mm) **or** size needed for gauge
Yarn needle

GAUGE: (5 dc, slip st) 4 times = 4¹/2"
Each Strip = 5" wide

STRIP (Make 9)
With Lt Purple, ch 214 **loosely**.

Rnd 1: 3 Sc in second ch from hook, sc in each ch across to last ch, 3 sc in last ch; working in free loops of beginning ch *(Fig. 31b, page 124)*, sc in each ch across; join with slip st to first sc: 428 sc.

Note: Loop a short piece of yarn around any stitch to mark Rnd 1 as **right** side.

Rnd 2: Ch 3 **(counts as first dc, now and throughout)**, working in Front Loops Only *(Fig. 32, page 124)*, (4 dc, slip st) in same st, (5 dc, slip st) in next st, (5 dc in next sc, skip next sc, slip st in next sc, skip next sc) 53 times, (5 dc, slip st) in each of next 2 sc, (5 dc in next sc, skip next sc, slip st in next sc, skip next sc) across; join with slip st to first dc, finish off: 110 5-dc groups.

Rnd 3: With **right** side facing and working in both loops, join Purple with slip st in slip st to right of last joining; working **behind** dc-groups, (ch 3, slip st in next slip st) around: 110 ch-3 sps.

To work **joining dc**, YO, insert hook in back ridge *(Fig. 26, page 122)* of center dc below same sp **and** in same sp, YO and pull up a loop, (YO and draw through 2 loops on hook) twice.

Rnd 4: Slip st in first ch-3 sp, ch 3, 2 dc in same sp, work joining dc, 3 dc in same sp as last 3 dc, slip st in next slip st, (3 dc in next ch-sp, work joining dc, 3 dc in same sp as last 3 dc, slip st in next slip st) twice, (2 dc in next ch-3 sp, work joining dc, 2 dc in same sp as last 2 dc, slip st in next slip st) 52 times, (3 dc in next ch-sp, work joining dc, 3 dc in same sp as last 3 dc, slip st in next slip st) 3 times, (2 dc in next ch-3 sp, work joining dc, 2 dc in same sp as last 2 dc, slip st in next slip st) across; join with slip st to first dc, finish off.

Rnd 5: With **right** side facing, join Dk Purple with slip st in slip st to right of last joining; working **behind** dc-groups, (ch 4, slip st in next slip st) around: 110 ch-4 sps.

Rnd 6: Repeat Rnd 4.

Rnd 7: With **right** side facing, join Black with slip st in slip st to right of last joining; (ch 6, skip next 7 dc, slip st in next slip st) 3 times, (ch 4, skip next 5 dc, slip st in next slip st) 52 times; ch 6, skip next 7 dc, (slip st in next slip st, ch 6, skip next 7 dc) twice, (slip st in next slip st, ch 4, skip next 5 dc) across; join with slip st to first slip st.

To work **joining sc**, insert hook in back ridge of center dc below same sp **and** in same sp, YO and pull up a loop, YO and draw through both loops on hook.

Rnd 8: Ch 1, sc in same st, place marker around last sc made for joining placement, † (5 sc in next loop, work joining sc, 5 sc in same sp as last 5 sc, sc in next slip st) 3 times, place marker around last sc made for joining placement †, (sc in next ch-4 sp, work joining sc, sc in same sp and in next sc) 52 times, place marker around last sc made for joining placement, repeat from † to † once, sc in next ch-4 sp, work joining sc, (sc in same sp and in next sc, sc in next ch-4 sp, work joining sc) across, sc in same sp; join with slip st to first sc, finish off.

ASSEMBLY
Place two Strips with **wrong** sides together. Using Black and working through both loops, whipstitch Strips together, beginning in first marked sc and ending in next marked sc *(Fig 33b, page 125)*.

Join remaining Strips in same manner, always working in same direction.

PRETTY POSTS

Rows of rosy shells form the center of each strip of this pretty afghan. Dark green front post stitches extend from the sides across creamy scallops to accent the Victorian-look throw.

Finished Size: 48" x 64"

MATERIALS
Worsted Weight Yarn:
    Red - 22 ounces, (620 grams, 1,005 yards)
    Cream - 12 ounces, (340 grams, 550 yards)
    Green - 30 ounces, (850 grams, 1,370 yards)
Crochet hook, size I (5.50 mm) **or** size needed for gauge
Yarn needle

GAUGE: Center = 2⅝" wide and 4 rows = 3"
             Each Strip = 6" wide

STITCH GUIDE

DOUBLE TREBLE CROCHET *(abbreviated dtr)*
YO 3 times, insert hook in st or sp indicated, YO and pull up a loop, (YO and draw through 2 loops on hook) 4 times *(Figs. 8a & b, page 117)*.
FRONT POST DOUBLE TREBLE CROCHET
  (abbreviated FPdtr)
YO 3 times, insert hook from **front** to **back** around post of st indicated, YO and pull up a loop *(Fig. 13, page 119)*, (YO and draw through 2 loops on hook) 4 times.

STRIP (Make 8)
CENTER
With Red, ch 11 **loosely**.

Row 1: Dc in fourth ch from hook **(3 skipped chs count as first dc)**, skip next 2 chs, 7 dc in next ch, skip next 2 chs, dc in last 2 chs: 11 dc.

Row 2 (Right side): Ch 3 **(counts as first dc, now and throughout)**, turn; dc in next dc, skip next 3 dc, 7 dc in next dc, skip next 3 dc, dc in last 2 dc.
Note: Loop a short piece of yarn around any stitch to mark Row 2 as **right** side and bottom edge.

Rows 3-76: Ch 3, turn; dc in next dc, skip next 3 dc, 7 dc in next dc, skip next 3 dc, dc in last 2 dc. Finish off.

END CAP
With **right** side facing and working in free loops of beginning ch *(Fig. 31b, page 124)*, join Red with slip st in ch at base of first dc; ch 3, dc in next ch, skip next 2 chs, 7 dc in next ch, skip next 2 chs, dc in last 2 chs; finish off.

BORDER
Rnd 1: With **right** side facing and working in end of rows, join Cream with slip st in End Cap; ch 3, 4 dc in same sp, (sc in next row, 5 dc in next row) across; working across last row, skip first 5 dc, 9 tr in next dc; working in end of rows, 5 dc in first row, (sc in next row, 5 dc in next row) across; working across End Cap, skip first 5 dc, 9 tr in next dc; join with slip st to first dc, finish off: 78 5-dc groups.

Rnd 2: With **right** side facing, join Green with slip st in BLO of center dc of first 5-dc group *(Fig. 32, page 124)*; ch 3, 4 dc in BLO of same st, † (working in **front** of next sc, dtr around dc **below** sc, skip next 2 dc, 5 dc in BLO of next dc) 38 times, working in 7-dc group on Row 76 of Center and in **front** of Rnd 1, skip first dc, dtr in **both** loops of next dc, skip next 2 tr on Rnd 1, 5 dc in BLO of next tr, skip next dc on Center and work FPdtr around next dc, skip next tr on Rnd 1, 5 dc in BLO of next tr, work FPdtr around same st as last FPdtr, skip next tr on Rnd 1, 5 dc in BLO of next tr, skip next dc on Center, dtr in **both** loops of next dc †, skip next 2 dc, 5 dc in BLO of next dc, repeat from † to † once; join with slip st to first dc: 84 5-dc groups.

Rnd 3: Working in both loops, slip st in next 2 dc, ch 1, sc in same st, (ch 2, skip next 2 dc, dc in next dtr, ch 2, skip next 2 dc, sc in next dc) 39 times, † ch 2, skip next 2 dc, 3 dc in next FPdtr, ch 1, skip next 2 dc, (dc, tr, 3 dtr, tr, dc) in next dc, ch 1, skip next 2 dc, 3 dc in next FPdtr, ch 2, skip next 2 dc, sc in next dc †, (ch 2, skip next 2 dc, dc in next dtr, ch 2, skip next 2 dc, sc in next dc) 40 times, repeat from † to † once, ch 2, skip next 2 dc, dc in next dtr, ch 2, skip last 2 dc; join with slip st to first sc: 168 ch-sps.

Rnd 4: Ch 1, working in sts and in chs, sc in same st and in next 230 sts, † 3 sc in next dc, place marker around center sc of 3-sc group just made for joining placement, sc in next 12 sts, 3 sc in next dtr, sc in next 12 sts, 3 sc in next dc, place marker around center sc of 3-sc group just made to mark joining placement †, sc in next 233 sts, repeat from † to † once, sc in last 2 chs; join with slip st to first sc, finish off.

ASSEMBLY
Place two Strips with **wrong** sides together and bottom edges at the same end. Using Green and working through inside loops only, whipstitch Strips together, beginning in first marked sc and ending in next marked sc *(Fig. 33a, page 125)*.

Join remaining Strips in same manner, always working in same direction.

LAVISH TEXTURE

An abundance of front post stitches gives this comfy afghan
its lavish texture. Brushed acrylic yarn provides feathery softness.

Finished Size: 45" x 63"

MATERIALS

Worsted Weight Brushed Acrylic Yarn:
51 ounces, (1,450 grams, 2,975 yards)
Crochet hook, size H (5.00 mm) **or** size needed for gauge

GAUGE: (dc, ch 1) 8 times = 3¹/₂"
Each Strip = 5" wide

STITCH GUIDE

CLUSTER
★ YO, insert hook in st or sp indicated, YO and pull up a loop, YO and draw through 2 loops on hook; repeat from ★ 2 times **more**; YO and draw through all 4 loops on hook *(Figs. 17a & b, page 120)*.
FRONT POST DOUBLE CROCHET
(abbreviated FPdc)
YO, insert hook from **front** to **back** around post of st indicated, YO and pull up a loop *(Fig. 11, page 118)*, (YO and draw through 2 loops on hook) twice.
FRONT POST CLUSTER *(abbreviated FPCluster)*
★ YO, insert hook from **front** to **back** around post of st indicated *(Fig. 9, page 118)*, YO and pull up a loop, YO and draw through 2 loops on hook; repeat from ★ 2 times **more**, YO and draw through all 4 loops on hook.

FIRST STRIP

Ch 194 **loosely**.
Rnd 1 (Right side)**:** (Dc, ch 1) 4 times in fifth ch from hook **(4 skipped chs count as first dc plus ch 1)**, † skip next 2 chs, (dc, ch 1) twice in next ch †, repeat from † to † across to last 3 chs, skip next 2 chs, (dc, ch 1) 5 times in last ch; working in free loops of beginning ch *(Fig. 31b, page 124)*, repeat from † to † across to last 2 chs, skip last 2 chs; join with slip st to first dc: 258 ch-1 sps.
Note: Loop a short piece of yarn around any stitch to mark Rnd 1 as **right** side.
Rnd 2: Slip st in first ch-1 sp, ch 2, (YO, insert hook in **same** sp, YO and pull up a loop, YO and draw through 2 loops on hook) twice, YO and draw through all 3 loops on hook, ch 2, (sc in next dc, ch 2, work Cluster in next ch-1 sp, ch 2) 3 times, (sc in next ch-1 sp, ch 2, work Cluster in next ch-1 sp, ch 2) 63 times, (sc in next dc, ch 2, work Cluster in next ch-1 sp, ch 2) 3 times, sc in next ch-1 sp, ch 2, (work Cluster in next ch-1 sp, ch 2, sc in next ch-1 sp, ch 2) across; join with slip st to top of first st: 132 Clusters.

Rnd 3: Ch 5, work FPdc around same Cluster, (ch 2, work FPdc) twice around next Cluster, ch 3, (work FPdc, ch 2) twice around each of next 65 Clusters, work (FPdc, ch 2, FPdc) around next Cluster, ch 3, (work FPdc, ch 2) twice around each Cluster across; join with slip st to third ch of beginning ch-5: 264 ch-sps.
Rnd 4: Slip st in first ch-2 sp, ch 1, sc in same sp, work FPCluster around next FPdc, ch 1, ★ sc in next sp, ch 1, work FPCluster around next st, ch 1; repeat from ★ around; join with slip st to first sc.
Rnd 5: Ch 1, sc in same st, ch 1, sc in next FPCluster, (ch 1, sc in next sc, ch 1, sc in next FPCluster) 6 times, (ch 1, skip next sc, sc in next FPCluster) 125 times, (ch 1, sc in next sc, ch 1, sc in next FPCluster) 7 times, ch 1, (skip next sc, sc in next FPCluster, ch 1) across; join with slip st to first sc: 278 ch-1 sps.
Rnd 6: Slip st in first ch-1 sp and in next sc, slip st in next ch-1 sp, † ch 2, 2 dc in next ch-1 sp, ch 4, slip st in top of last dc made, 2 dc in next ch-1 sp, ch 2, slip st in next ch-1 sp †, repeat from † to † 2 times **more**, (ch 4, skip next ch-1 sp, slip st in next ch-1 sp) 65 times, repeat from † to † 3 times, ch 4, skip next ch-1 sp, (slip st in next ch-1 sp, ch 4, skip next ch-1 sp) across; join with slip st to slip st to base of beginning ch-2, finish off.

REMAINING 8 STRIPS

Work same as First Strip through Rnd 5.
Rnd 6 (Joining rnd)**:** Slip st in first ch-1 sp and in next sc, slip st in next ch-1 sp, † ch 2, 2 dc in next ch-1 sp, ch 4, slip st in top of last dc made, 2 dc in next ch-1 sp, ch 2, slip st in next ch-1 sp †, repeat from † to † 2 times **more**, (ch 4, skip next ch-1 sp, slip st in next ch-1 sp) 65 times, repeat from † to † 3 times, ch 4, skip next ch-1 sp, slip st in next ch-1 sp, ch 2, holding Strips with **wrong** sides together, slip st in corresponding ch-4 sp on **previous Strip** *(Fig. 28, page 122)*, ch 2, skip next ch-1 sp on **new Strip**, slip st in next ch-1 sp, ★ ch 2, slip st in next ch-4 sp on **previous Strip**, ch 2, skip next ch-1 sp on **new Strip**, slip st in next ch-1 sp; repeat from ★ across to last ch-1 sp, ch 4, skip last ch-1 sp; join with slip st to slip st to base of beginning ch-2, finish off.

TEATIME ELEGANCE

Zigzags of double treble clusters and shells cascade over green double crochets on this snuggly afghan. Simple stitches of rose-petal pink finish the lovely wrap.

Finished Size: 45" x 66"

MATERIALS
Worsted Weight Yarn:
Bone - 26 ounces, (740 grams, 1,520 yards)
Green - 22 ounces, (620 grams, 1,285 yards)
Rose - 11 ounces, (310 grams, 645 yards)
Crochet hook, size I (5.50 mm) **or** size needed for gauge

GAUGE: Center = 1³/₄" wide and 6 rows = 4¹/₂"
Each Strip = 5" wide

STITCH GUIDE

CLUSTER
★ YO, insert hook in **next** dc, YO and pull up a loop, YO and draw through 2 loops on hook; repeat from ★ 2 times **more**, YO and draw through all 4 loops on hook.

FRONT POST DOUBLE TREBLE CROCHET
(abbreviated FPdtr)
YO 3 times, insert hook from **front** to **back** around post of dc **below** next dc, YO and pull up a loop *(Fig. 13, page 119)*, (YO and draw through 2 loops on hook) 4 times.

DTR CLUSTER
YO 3 times, working in end of rows of Center, insert hook in same sp and to **right** of 3-dc on Rnd 1 **below** last 3 sc made, YO and pull up a loop, (YO and draw through 2 loops on hook) 3 times, YO 3 times, skip next 6 dc on Rnd 1, insert hook in same sp and to **left** of last skipped dc, YO and pull up a loop, (YO and draw through 2 loops on hook) 3 times, YO and draw through all 3 loops on hook. Do **not** skip st behind dtr Cluster *(Figs. 18a & b, page 120)*.

STRIP (Make 9)
CENTER
With Bone, ch 6; join with slip st to form a ring.
Row 1 (Right side): Ch 3 **(counts as first dc, now and throughout)**, 7 dc in ring: 8 dc.
Note: Loop a short piece of yarn around any stitch to mark Row 1 as **right** side and bottom edge.
Rows 2-79: Ch 3, turn; skip next dc, 6 dc in next dc, skip next 4 dc, dc in last dc.
Row 80: Ch 3, turn; work Cluster, ch 3, work Cluster, dc in last dc; finish off.

BORDER
Rnd 1: With **right** side facing, join Green with slip st in ch-3 sp on last row; ch 3, 8 dc in same sp; working in end of rows, 3 dc in each row across; 9 dc in beginning ring; working in end of rows, 3 dc in each row across; join with slip st to first dc: 498 dc.
Rnd 2: Ch 3, dc in same st, 2 dc in each of next 8 dc, dc in each dc across to next 9-dc group, 2 dc in each of next 9 dc, dc in each dc across; with Bone, join with slip st to first dc *(Fig. 30b, page 124)*: 516 dc.
Rnd 3: Ch 1, sc in same st, † (work FPdtr, skip dc behind FPdtr, sc in next dc) 4 times, work FPdtr, do **not** skip st behind FPdtr, (sc in next dc, work FPdtr, skip dc behind FPdtr) 4 times, sc in next 4 dc, work dtr Cluster, (sc in next 6 dc, work dtr Cluster) 39 times †, sc in next 4 dc, repeat from † to † once, sc in last 3 dc; with Rose, join with slip st to first sc: 598 sts.
Rnd 4: Ch 1, sc in same st, † 2 sc in next FPdtr, (sc in next st, 2 sc in next FPdtr) 3 times, 2 dc in next sc, dc in next FPdtr, 2 dc in next sc, 2 sc in next FPdtr, (sc in next sc, 2 sc in next FPdtr) 3 times, sc in next 4 sc, skip next st, (sc in next 6 sc, skip next st) 39 times †, sc in next 4 sc, repeat from † to † once, sc in last 3 sc; join with slip st to Back Loop Only of first sc: 538 sts.
Rnd 5: Ch 1, working in Back Loops Only, sc in same st, † place marker around last sc made for joining placement, sc in same st and in next 13 sts, 3 sc in next dc, sc in next 13 sts, 2 sc in next sc, place marker around last sc made for joining placement †, sc in next 241 sc, repeat from † to † once, sc in each sc across; join with slip st to both loops of first sc, finish off.

ASSEMBLY
Place two Strips with **wrong** sides together and bottom edges at the same end. Using Rose and working through inside loops only, whipstitch Strips together, beginning in first marked sc and ending in next marked sc *(Fig. 33a, page 125)*.

Join remaining Strips in same manner, always working in same direction.

CLOUD-SOFT SHELLS

Fashioned with lacy shell stitches and soft scallops, this dreamy afghan will make you feel as if you're lying on a blanket of clouds. The airy openwork makes it a summertime favorite.

Finished Size: 45" x 65"

MATERIALS
Worsted Weight Yarn:
    43 ounces, (1,220 grams, 2,510 yards)
Crochet hook, size I (5.50 mm) **or** size needed for gauge
Yarn needle

GAUGE: Center = 2³/₈" wide and 8 rows = 5"
             Each Strip = 4¹/₂" wide

STRIP (Make 10)
CENTER
Ch 11 **loosely**.
Row 1 (Right side)**:** Dc in fourth ch from hook **(3 skipped chs count as first dc)**, ch 1, skip next 2 chs, 4 dc in next ch, ch 1, skip next 2 chs, dc in last 2 chs: 8 dc.
Note: Loop a short piece of yarn around any stitch to mark Row 1 as **right** side and bottom edge.

Row 2: Ch 3 **(counts as first dc, now and throughout),** turn; dc in next dc, ch 2, skip next 2 dc, 2 dc in sp **before** next dc **(Fig. 27, page 122)**, ch 2, skip next 2 dc, dc in last 2 dc.
Row 3: Ch 3, turn; dc in next dc, ch 1, skip next dc, 4 dc in sp **before** next dc, ch 1, skip next dc, dc in last 2 dc.
Rows 4-101: Repeat Rows 2 and 3, 49 times.
Do **not** finish off.

BORDER
Ch 3, working in end of rows, (4 dc, sc, 5 dc) in first row, sc in next row, (5 dc in next row, sc in next row) across to last row, 5 dc in last row, place marker in center dc of last 5-dc group made for Trim placement, (sc, 5 dc) in same row; working around beginning ch, skip first 4 dc, (sc, 7 dc, sc) in sp **before** next dc; working in end of rows, (5 dc, sc, 5 dc) in first row, sc in next row, (5 dc in next row, sc in next row) across to last row, 5 dc in last row, place marker around center dc of last 5-dc group made for Trim placement, (sc, 5 dc) in same row; working across last row, skip first 4 dc, (sc, 7 dc, sc) in sp **before** next dc; join with slip st to first dc, finish off.

TRIM
FIRST SIDE
Row 1: With **wrong** side facing, join yarn with slip st in marked st; ch 1, sc in same st, (ch 4, sc in center dc of next 5-dc group) 50 times: 50 ch-4 sps.
Row 2: Ch 1, turn; sc in each sc and in each ch across; finish off: 251 sc.
SECOND SIDE
Work same as First Side.

ASSEMBLY
Place two Strips with **wrong** sides together and bottom edges at the same end. Working through both loops, whipstitch Strips together, beginning in first sc of Trim and ending in last sc **(Fig. 33b, page 125)**.

Join remaining Strips in same manner, always working in same direction.

HANDSOME CLASSIC

*Ideal for the den or study, this handsome afghan features a cross
pattern worked in rounds. The centers are stitched in variegated yarn,
and borders of black and gray complete the classic design.*

Finished Size: 45" x 61"

MATERIALS
Worsted Weight Yarn:
    Gray - 18 ounces, (510 grams, 1,235 yards)
    Black - 16 ounces, (450 grams, 1,100 yards)
    Variegated - 13 ounces, (370 grams, 895 yards)
Crochet hook, size H (5.00 mm) **or** size needed for gauge
Yarn needle

GAUGE: Center = 2¹/₂" wide
              Each Strip = 4¹/₂" wide

STRIP (Make 10)
FIRST CROSS
Rnd 1 (Right side): With Variegated, ch 4, 2 dc in fourth
ch from hook **(3 skipped chs count as first dc, now and
throughout)**, ch 3, (3 dc in same ch, ch 3) 3 times; join
with slip st to first dc: 12 dc and 4 ch-3 sps.
Note: Loop a short piece of yarn around any stitch to mark
Rnd 1 as **right** side.
Rnd 2: Ch 3 **(counts as first dc, now and throughout)**, dc
in next 2 dc, (dc, ch 3, dc) in next ch-3 sp, ★ dc in next
3 dc, (dc, ch 3, dc) in next ch-3 sp; repeat from ★ around;
join with slip st to first dc, do **not** finish off: 20 dc.

NEXT 13 CROSSES
Rnd 1: Slip st in next dc, ch 13, (2 dc, ch 3, 3 dc, ch 3,
dc) in fourth ch from hook, slip st in seventh ch from
previous Cross (counts as one dc, now and throughout),
(dc, ch 3, 3 dc) in same ch on **new Cross**, ch 3; join with
slip st to first dc: 12 dc and 4 ch-3 sps.
Note: Mark Rnd 1 as **right** side.
Rnd 2: Ch 3, dc in next 2 dc, (dc, ch 3, dc) in next ch-3 sp,
dc in next 3 dc, (dc, ch 3, dc) in next ch-3 sp, dc in next
dc, slip st in fourth ch from **previous Cross**, dc in next dc
on **new Cross**, (dc, ch 3, dc) in next ch-3 sp, dc in next
3 dc, (dc, ch 3, dc) in last ch-3 sp; join with slip st to
first dc, do **not** finish off: 20 dc.

LAST CROSS
Rnd 1: Slip st in next dc, ch 13, (2 dc, ch 3, 3 dc, ch 3,
dc) in fourth ch from hook, slip st in seventh ch from
previous Cross, (dc, ch 3, 3 dc) in same ch on **new Cross**,
ch 3; join with slip st to first dc: 12 dc and 4 ch-3 sps.
Note: Mark Rnd 1 as **right** side.
Rnd 2: Ch 3, dc in next 2 dc, (dc, ch 3, dc) in next ch-3 sp,
dc in next 3 dc, (dc, ch 3, dc) in next ch-3 sp, dc in next
dc, slip st in fourth ch from **previous Cross**, dc in next dc
on **new Cross**, (dc, ch 3, dc) in next ch-3 sp, dc in next 3 dc,
(dc, ch 3, dc) in last ch-3 sp; join with slip st to first dc,
finish off: 15 Crosses.

BORDER
To work **double treble crochet (abbreviated dtr)**, YO 3
times, working in **front** of next ch-3, insert hook in ch-3 sp
indicated, YO and pull up a loop, (YO and draw through
2 loops on hook) 4 times *(Figs. 8a & b, page 117)*.
Rnd 1: With **right** side facing and holding Crosses
vertically, join Black with slip st in first st to **right** of last
joining; ch 3, dc in next 4 dc, ✝ dtr in next ch-3 sp on rnd
below, (dc, ch 3, dc) in next ch-3 sp, dtr in same sp as
last dtr made, dc in next 5 dc, dtr in next ch-3 sp on rnd
below, (dc, ch 3, dc) in next ch-3 sp, dtr in same sp as
last dtr made, slip st in next dc, skip next dc, being careful
not to twist ch, 3 dc around ch between Crosses, skip next
dc, slip st in next dc ✝, repeat from ✝ to ✝ 13 times **more**,
dtr in next ch-3 sp on rnd **below**, (dc, ch 3, dc) in next
ch-3 sp, dtr in same sp as last dtr made, [dc in next 5 dc,
dtr in next ch-3 sp on rnd **below**, (dc, ch 3, dc) in next
ch-3 sp, dtr in same sp as last dtr made] 3 times, ★ slip st in
next dc, skip next dc, working around ch between Crosses,
dc **between** lower loops of next 3 dc *(Fig. 22, page 121)*,
skip next dc, slip st in next dc, dtr in next ch-3 sp on rnd
below, (dc, ch 3, dc) in next ch-3 sp, dtr in same sp as last
dtr made, dc in next 5 dc, dtr in next ch-3 sp on rnd
below, (dc, ch 3, dc) in next ch-3 sp, dtr in same sp as
last dtr made; repeat from ★ across; join with slip st to
first dc, finish off.

To **decrease**, ★ YO insert hook in **next** dc, YO and pull up a loop, YO and draw through 2 loops on hook; repeat from ★ 2 times **more**, YO and draw through all 4 loops on hook.
Rnd 2: With **right** side facing, join Gray with slip st in first dc to left of last ch-3 sp made; ch 3, dc in next 8 sts, dtr in next ch-3 sp on rnd **below**, (dc, ch 3, dc) in next ch-3 sp, dtr in same sp as last dtr made, † dc in next 9 sts, dtr in next ch-3 sp on rnd **below**, (dc, ch 3, dc) in next ch-3 sp, dtr in same ch-3 sp as last dtr made, slip st in next dc, skip next 2 sts, decrease, skip next 2 sts, slip st in next dc, dtr in next ch-3 sp on rnd **below**, dc in next ch-3 sp, ch 1, slip st in last ch-3 sp made (*Fig. 25, page 122*), ch 1, dc in same sp as last dc made, dtr in same sp as last dtr made †, repeat from † to † 13 times **more**, [dc in next 9 sts, dtr in next ch-3 sp on rnd **below**, (dc, ch 3, dc) in next

ch-3 sp, dtr in same sp as last dtr made] 3 times, slip st in next dc, skip next 2 sts, decrease, skip next 2 sts, slip st in next dc, dtr in next ch-3 sp on rnd **below**, dc in next ch-3 sp, ch 1, slip st in last ch-3 sp made, ch 1, dc in same sp as last dc made, dtr in same sp as last dtr made, repeat from † to † 13 times, dc in next 9 sts, dtr in ch-3 sp on rnd **below**, (dc, ch 3, dc) in next ch-3 sp, dtr in same sp as last dtr made; join with slip st to first dc, finish off.

ASSEMBLY

Place two Strips with **wrong** sides together. Using Gray and working through both loops, whipstitch Strips together, beginning in center ch of first corner and ending in center ch of next corner (*Fig. 33b, page 125*).

Join remaining Strips in same manner, always working in same direction.

TERRIFIC TWISTS

A twist effect creates waves of texture on this terrific afghan. Stitched in two shades of teal, the wrap will lend a tranquil ambience to your home.

Finished Size: 49" x 66"

MATERIALS
Worsted Weight Yarn:
  Teal - 27 ounces, (770 grams, 1,855 yards)
  Dk Teal - 28 ounces, (800 grams, 1,920 yards)
Crochet hook, size G (4.00 mm) **or** size needed for gauge

GAUGE: 17 sts = 4"
  Each Strip = 3¼ " wide

FIRST STRIP
With Dk Teal, ch 274 **loosely**.
Rnd 1 (Right side): (Dc, ch 1, dc) in fifth ch from hook **(4 skipped chs count as first dc plus ch 1)**, (ch 1, skip next ch, dc in next 3 chs) across to last ch, (ch 1, dc) 3 times in last ch; working in free loops of beginning ch and in skipped chs (*Fig. 31b, page 124*), (ch 1, skip next ch, dc in next 3 chs) 67 times, ch 1; join with slip st to first dc, finish off: 140 ch-1 sps.
Note: Loop a short piece of yarn around any stitch to mark Rnd 1 as **right** side.

To work **Long double treble crochet (abbreviated Long dtr)**, YO 3 times, working in **front** of previous sts, insert hook from **back** to **front** in sp or st indicated, YO and pull up a loop, (YO and draw through 2 loops on hook) 4 times.

Rnd 2: With **right** side facing, join Teal with slip st in same st as joining; ch 3 **(counts as first dc, now and throughout)**, 2 dc in same st, work Long dtr in ch-1 sp before 3-dc group just made, (3 dc in next dc, work Long dtr in ch-1 sp **before** 3-dc group just made) twice, (dc in next 3 dc, work Long dtr in ch-1 sp **before** 3 dc just made) 67 times, (3 dc in next dc, work Long dtr in ch-1 sp **before** 3-dc group just made) 3 times, (dc in next 3 dc, work Long dtr in ch-1 sp **before** 3 dc just made) across; join with slip st to first dc, finish off: 140 Long dtr.
Rnd 3: With **right** side facing, join Dk Teal with slip st in same st as joining; ch 3, dc in next 2 dc, work Long dtr in Long dtr **before** 3 dc just made, ch 1, ★ dc in next 3 dc, work Long dtr in Long dtr **before** 3 dc just made, ch 1; repeat from ★ around; join with slip st to first dc, finish off.

SECOND STRIP
Reversing colors, work same as First Strip through Rnd 2.
Rnd 3 (Joining rnd): With **right** side facing, join Teal with slip st in same st as joining; ch 3, dc in next 2 dc, work Long dtr in Long dtr **before** 3 dc just made, ★ ch 1, dc in next 3 dc, work Long dtr in Long dtr **before** 3 dc just made; repeat from ★ 71 times **more**, holding Strips with **wrong** sides together, slip st in corresponding ch-1 sp on **previous Strip** (*Fig. 28, page 122*), (dc in next 3 dc on **new Strip**, work Long dtr in Long dtr **before** 3 dc just made, slip st in next ch-1 sp on **previous Strip**) 67 times; join with slip st to first dc, finish off.

THIRD STRIP
Work same as First Strip through Rnd 2.
Rnd 3 (Joining rnd)**:** With Dk Teal, work same as Second Strip.

REMAINING 12 STRIPS
Repeat Second and Third Strips, 6 times.

GENTLEMAN'S CHOICE

*Shell stitches worked in alternating colors of natural
and navy give our wrap contrasting interest. Striking front post
double treble crochets enhance this gentleman's throw.*

Finished Size: 47¹/₂" x 67"

MATERIALS
Worsted Weight Yarn:
Navy - 23 ounces, (650 grams, 1,450 yards)
Natural - 30 ounces, (850 grams, 1,890 yards)
Crochet hook, size J (6.00 mm) **or** size needed for gauge
Yarn needle

GAUGE: Center = 2¹/₄" wide and 4 rows = 2¹/₂"
Each Strip = 4³/₄" wide

STRIP (Make 10)
CENTER
With Navy, ch 11 **loosely**.
Row 1: Dc in fourth ch from hook **(3 skipped chs count as first dc)**, skip next 2 chs, 5 dc in next ch, skip next 2 chs, dc in last 2 chs.
Row 2 (Right side)**:** Ch 3 **(counts as first dc, now and throughout)**, turn; dc in next dc, skip next 2 dc, 5 dc in next dc, skip next 2 dc, dc in last 2 dc changing to Natural in last dc **(Fig. 30a, page 124)**.
Note: Loop a short piece of yarn around any stitch to mark Row 2 as **right** side and bottom edge.
Row 3: Ch 3, turn; dc in next dc, skip next 2 dc, 5 dc in next dc, skip next 2 dc, dc in last 2 dc.
Row 4: Ch 3, turn; dc in next dc, skip next 2 dc, 5 dc in next dc, skip next 2 dc, dc in last 2 dc changing to Navy in last dc.
Row 5: Ch 3, turn; dc in next dc, skip next 2 dc, 5 dc in next dc, skip next 2 dc, dc in last 2 dc.
Rows 6-101: Repeat Rows 2-5, 24 times.
Row 102: Ch 3, turn; dc in next dc, skip next 2 dc, 5 dc in next dc, skip next 2 dc, dc in last 2 dc; do **not** finish off.

BORDER
Rnd 1: Ch 3, working in end of rows, 2 dc in end of each row across to last row, 3 dc in last row; working in free loops of beginning ch **(Fig. 31b, page 124)**, dc in ch below second dc, skip next 2 chs, 5 dc in next ch, skip next 2 chs, dc in next ch; working in end of rows, 3 dc in first row, 2 dc in end of each row across to last row, 3 dc in last row; working across Row 102, skip first dc, dc in next dc, skip next 2 dc, 5 dc in next dc, skip next 2 dc, dc in next dc; with Natural, join with slip st to first dc: 426 dc.

To work **double treble crochet (abbreviated dtr)**, YO 3 times, insert hook in st indicated, YO and pull up a loop, (YO and draw through 2 loops on hook) 4 times **(Figs. 8a & b, page 117)**.
Rnd 2: Ch 3, dc in same st, 2 dc in each of next 2 dc, dc in next 2 dc, dtr around end of first Natural 5-dc group on Center **(Fig. 23, page 121)**, dc in next 2 dc, (dtr around end of next 5-dc group on Center, dc in next 2 dc) 98 times, 2 dc in each of next 3 dc, dc in next dc, dtr around end of 5-dc group on Row 1 of Center, 2 dc in each of next 5 dc, dtr around free end of 5-dc group on Row 1 of Center, dc in next dc, 2 dc in each of next 3 dc, dc in next 2 dc, (dtr around end of next 5-dc group on Center, dc in next 2 dc) 99 times, 2 dc in each of next 3 dc, dc in next dc, dtr around end of next 5-dc group on Row 101 of Center, 2 dc in each of next 5 dc, dtr around free end of 5-dc group on Row 101 of Center, dc in next dc; with Navy, join with slip st to first dc: 202 dtr.
Rnd 3: Ch 1, working in Back Loops Only **(Fig. 32, page 124)**, sc in same st and in next 3 dc, † place marker around last sc made for joining placement, sc in next 4 dc, skip next dtr, (sc in next 2 dc, skip next dtr) 98 times, sc in next 5 dc, place marker around last sc made for joining placement, sc in next 4 dc, skip next dtr, sc in next 3 dc, 2 sc in each of next 4 dc, sc in next 3 dc, skip next dtr †, sc in next 5 dc, repeat from † to † once, sc in last dc; join with slip st to both loops of first sc, finish off.

ASSEMBLY
Place two Strips with **wrong** sides together and bottom edges at the same end. Using Navy and working through inside loops only, whipstitch Strips together, beginning in first marked sc and ending in next marked sc **(Fig. 33a, page 125)**.

Join remaining Strips in same manner, always working in same direction.

SUMMER SHERBET

As delightful as a dip of icy sherbet on a hot summer day, this pastel pretty is a visual treat! Double crochets worked in rosy pink create a textured overlay around a foundation row of green double crochets and post stitches.

Finished Size: 49" x 70"

MATERIALS
Worsted Weight Yarn:
Green - 18 ounces, (510 grams, 1,185 yards)
Lt Rose - 20 ounces, (570 grams, 1,315 yards)
Rose - 20¹/2 ounces, (580 grams, 1,345 yards)
Crochet hook, size G (4.00 mm) **or** size needed for gauge
Yarn needle

GAUGE: 16 dc and 8 rows = 4"
Each Strip = 3³/4" wide

STRIP (Make 13)
CENTER
With Green, ch 266 **loosely**.
Foundation Row (Right side)**:** Dc in fourth ch from hook and in each ch across; finish off: 264 sts.
Note: Loop a short piece of yarn around any stitch to mark Foundation Row as **right** side.

TRIM
FIRST SIDE
To work **Front Post double crochet (abbreviated FPdc)**, YO, insert hook from **front** to **back** around post of st indicated, YO and pull up a loop *(Fig. 11, page 118)*, (YO and draw through 2 loops on hook) twice.
With **right** side facing, join Green with slip st in top of beginning ch; ch 2, ★ work FPdc around next dc, skip dc behind FPdc, hdc in next 2 dc; repeat from ★ across to last 2 dc, work FPdc around next dc, skip dc behind FPdc, hdc in last dc; finish off: 88 FPdc.
SECOND SIDE
With **right** side facing and working in free loops of beginning ch *(Fig. 31b, page 124)*, join Green with slip st in first ch; ch 2, work FPdc around next dc (same dc as FPdc on opposite side), ★ skip ch behind FPdc, hdc in next 2 chs, work FPdc around next dc; repeat from ★ 86 times **more**, skip ch behind FPdc, hdc in next ch; finish off: 88 FPdc.

BORDER
Rnd 1: With **right** side facing, join Lt Rose with slip st in top of beginning ch on First Side of Trim; ch 4, place marker around ch-4 just made for Rnd 2 joining, tr in next st and in each st across; working in end of rows, 4 tr in first row, 3 tr in Foundation Row, 4 tr in next row, tr in each st across Second Side; working in end of rows, 4 tr in first row, 3 tr in Foundation Row, 4 tr in next row; join with slip st to top of beginning ch-4; finish off: 550 sts.
Rnd 2: With **right** side facing, join Rose with slip st in marked st; ch 2, place marker around last ch-2 made for joining placement, † hdc in next 264 tr, place marker around last hdc made for joining placement, hdc in same tr, 2 hdc in each of next 10 tr †, hdc in next tr, place marker around last hdc made for joining placement, repeat from † to † once; join with slip st to top of beginning ch-2, finish off: 572 sts.

OVERLAY
With **right** side of long end facing and working around post of each FPdc, join Rose with slip st around first FPdc on First Side of Trim; ch 3, 2 dc around same FPdc, † 3 dc around next FPdc and around each FPdc across, 5 dc around second st on Foundation Row (at base of FPdc) †; working across Second Side, repeat from † to † once; join with slip st to top of beginning ch-3, finish off.

ASSEMBLY
Place two Strips with **wrong** sides together. Using Rose and working through inside loops only, whipstitch Strips together, beginning in first marked st and ending in next marked st *(Fig. 33a, page 125)*.

Join remaining Strips in same manner, always working in same direction.

TRAILING DIAMONDS

Bright teal stitches outline vibrant pink clusters to create the look of trailing diamonds on this cover-up. A simple black border creates dramatic results!

Finished Size: 47" x 63"

MATERIALS
Worsted Weight Yarn:
Black - 21 ounces, (600 grams, 1,440 yards)
Pink - 14 ounces, (400 grams, 960 yards)
Teal - 18 ounces, (510 grams, 1,235 yards)
Crochet hook, size H (5.00 mm) **or** size needed for gauge
Yarn needle

GAUGE: Center = 2" wide and 5 rows = 3"
Each Strip = 4¹/4" wide

STRIP (Make 11)
CENTER
To work **Cluster**, ★ YO, insert hook in ch or sp indicated, YO and pull up a loop, YO and draw through 2 loops on hook; repeat from ★ once **more**, YO and draw through all 3 loops on hook *(Figs. 17a & b, page 120)*.
With Pink, ch 11 **loosely**.
Row 1 (Right side): Dc in fourth ch from hook **(3 skipped chs count as first dc)**, skip next 2 chs, work (Cluster, ch 1, Cluster) in next ch, skip next 2 chs, dc in last 2 chs.
Note: Loop a short piece of yarn around any stitch to mark Row 1 as **right** side and bottom edge.
Rows 2-101: Ch 3 **(counts as first dc, now and throughout)**, turn; dc in next dc, work (Cluster, ch 1, Cluster) in next ch-1 sp, dc in last 2 dc.
Finish off.

BORDER
To work **double treble crochet (abbreviated dtr)**, YO 3 times, insert hook in st or sp indicated, YO and pull up a loop, (YO and draw through 2 loops on hook) 4 times *(Figs. 8a & b, page 117)*.
Rnd 1: With **right** side facing and working in end rows, join Teal with slip st in last row; ch 3, working in **front** of dc, (dtr, ch 1, dtr) around first Cluster on **same** row, [dc in next row, working in **front** of dc, (dtr, ch 1, dtr) around first Cluster on next row] across, dc in same row as last dtr, working in free loops of beginning ch *(Fig. 31b, page 124)*, skip first 4 chs, 7 dtr in next ch; working in end of rows, dc in first row, working in **front** of dc, (dtr, ch 1, dtr) around first Cluster on same row, [dc in next row, working in **front** of dc, (dtr, ch 1, dtr) around first Cluster on next row] across, dc in same row as last dtr, 7 dtr in ch-1 sp on last row; with Black, join with slip st to first dc.
Rnd 2: Ch 3, working in Back Loops Only *(Fig. 32, page 124)*, dc in next dtr, † working in **front** of next ch-1 and in end of rows on Center, 3 dtr in row **below** ch-1, (skip next dtr, dc in next dc, working in **front** of next ch-1, 3 dtr in row **below** ch-1) 50 times, dc in next 2 sts, 2 dc in each of next 3 dtr, 5 tr in next dtr, 2 dc in each of next 3 dtr †, dc in next 2 sts, repeat from † to † once; join with slip st to first dc: 102 3-dtr groups.
Rnd 3: Ch 1, working in Back Loops Only, 2 sc in same st, † place marker around last sc made for joining placement, sc in next 206 sts, place marker around last sc made for joining placement, sc in same st, (sc in next st, 2 sc in next st) 4 times, 3 sc in next tr †, 2 sc in next tr, (sc in next st, 2 sc in next st) 4 times, repeat from † to † once, (2 sc in next tr, sc in next tr) 4 times; join with slip st to first sc, finish off.

ASSEMBLY
Place two Strips with **wrong** sides and bottom edges at the same end. Using Black and working through inside loops only, whipstitch two Strips together, beginning in first marked sc and ending in next marked sc *(Fig. 33a, page 125)*.

Join remaining Strips in same manner, always working in same direction.

On this sweet afghan for baby, pink strips featuring braided chain loops are finished with a simple white edging. The cozy cover-up is destined to become a cherished keepsake.

Finished Size: 31" x 40"

MATERIALS
Sport Weight Yarn:
Pink - 9 ounces, (260 grams, 850 yards)
White - 7 ounces, (200 grams, 660 yards)
Crochet hook, size G (4.00 mm) **or** size needed for gauge

GAUGE: 16 dc and 8 rows = 4"
Each Strip = 3³/4" wide

STITCH GUIDE

CHAIN LOOP *(abbreviated Ch Loop)*
Ch 10, slip st in top of dc just made.
JOINING DC
YO, insert hook in next dc, YO and pull up a loop, YO and draw through 2 loops on hook, insert hook in Ch Loop, YO and draw through Ch Loop **and** both loops on hook.
DECREASE (uses next 2 dc)
★ YO, insert hook in **next** dc, YO and pull up a loop, YO and draw through 2 loops on hook; repeat from ★ once **more**, YO and draw through all 3 loops on hook **(counts as one dc).**

STRIP (Make 8)
CENTER
Row 1 (Right side): With Pink, ch 4, dc in fourth ch from hook: 2 sts.
Note: Loop a short piece of yarn around any stitch to mark Row 1 as **right** side and bottom edge.
Row 2: Ch 3 **(counts as first dc, now and throughout),** turn; dc in same st, 2 dc in top of beginning ch: 4 dc.
Note: When working remaining rows, hold Ch Loops on **right** side of work.
Row 3: Ch 3, turn; dc in same st and in next dc, work Ch Loop, dc in next dc, 2 dc in last dc: 6 dc.
Row 4: Ch 3, turn; dc in same st and in next 2 dc, work Ch Loop, dc in next 2 dc, 2 dc in last dc: 8 dc.
Row 5: Ch 3, turn; dc in same st and in next 3 dc, work Ch Loop, dc in next 3 dc, 2 dc in last dc: 10 dc.
Rows 6-74: Ch 3, turn; dc in next 4 dc, work Ch Loop, dc in last 5 dc.

Row 75: Ch 3, turn; decrease, dc in next 5 dc, decrease: 8 dc.
Note: Working from bottom to top, braid Ch Loops beginning on Row 3 as follows: insert hook from **front** to **back** in first Ch Loop, ★ pull next Ch Loop through Ch Loop on hook; repeat from ★ across, leaving last Ch Loop free for joining.
Row 76 (Joining row): Ch 3, turn; decrease, work joining dc, dc in next 2 dc, decrease: 6 dc.
Row 77: Ch 3, turn; decrease, dc in next dc, decrease: 4 dc.
Row 78: Ch 3, turn; decrease, dc in last dc: 3 dc.
Row 79: Ch 3, turn; skip next dc, dc in last dc; finish off: 2 dc.

BORDER
Rnd 1: With **right** side facing and working in end of rows, join White with slip st in Row 79; ch 1, 5 sc in same row, 2 sc in each row across to Row 1, 5 sc in Row 1, 2 sc in end of each row across; join with slip st to first sc: 318 sc.
Rnd 2: Slip st in next 2 sc, ch 3, 8 dc in same st, skip next 2 sc, (3 dc in next sc, skip next 2 sc) 52 times, 9 dc in next sc, skip next 2 sc, (3 dc in next sc, skip next 2 sc) across; join with slip st to first dc, finish off: 52 3-dc groups **each** side.

ASSEMBLY
Place two Strips side by side with **right** sides facing and bottom edges at the same end. Skip first three 3-dc groups on left Strip and join White with slip st in next dc; skip first three 3-dc groups on right Strip, inserting hook from **right** to **wrong** side of work, slip st in next dc, ★ slip st in next dc on left Strip, slip st in next dc on right Strip; repeat from ★ across to last three 3-dc groups on both Strips, leave remaining dc unworked; finish off.

Join remaining Strips in same manner, always working in same direction.

EDGING
With **right** side facing, join White with slip st in center dc of 9-dc group at top right corner, ★ [ch 4, skip next dc, (slip st in next dc, ch 4, skip next dc) across to next joining, slip st in joining] 7 times, (ch 4, skip next dc, slip st in next dc) 13 times, ch 4, skip next 2 dc, slip st in next dc; repeat from ★ once **more**, ch 4, skip next dc, (slip st in next dc, ch 4, skip next dc) around; join with slip st to first slip st, finish off.

FANCIFUL SCULPTURE

Layers of sculptured shell stitches give this afghan elegant texture. Worked in rich blue, the wrap is strikingly beautiful!

Finished Size: 45" x 66"

MATERIALS
Worsted Weight Yarn:
35 ounces, (1,000 grams, 2,300 yards)
Crochet hook, size I (5.50 mm) **or** size needed for gauge

GAUGE: In pattern, 5 dc, Shell = 2¹/2"
Each Strip = 4¹/2" wide

STITCH GUIDE

SHELL
(2 Dc, ch 2, 2 dc) in st or sp indicated.
BACK POST HALF DOUBLE CROCHET
(abbreviated BPhdc)
YO, insert hook from **back** to **front** around post of st indicated, YO and pull up a loop *(Fig. 14, page 119)*, YO and draw through all 3 loops on hook. Skip st in front of BPhdc.
BACK POST DOUBLE CROCHET
(abbreviated BPdc)
YO, insert hook from **back** to **front** around post of st indicated, YO and pull up a loop *(Fig. 15, page 119)*, (YO and draw through 2 loops on hook) twice. Skip st in front of BPdc.

FIRST STRIP
Ch 200 **loosely.**
Rnd 1 (Right side): (Dc, ch 1, 2 dc, ch 1, dc) in fourth ch from hook, † dc in next 4 chs, skip next ch, work Shell in next ch, ★ skip next ch, dc in next 5 chs, skip next ch, work Shell in next ch; repeat from ★ 22 times **more**, skip next ch, dc in next 4 chs †, [dc, ch 1, (2 dc, ch 1) twice, dc] in last ch, working in free loops of beginning ch *(Fig. 31b, page 124)*, repeat from † to † once, dc in same ch as first dc, ch 1; join with slip st to top of beginning ch: 48 Shells.
Note: Loop a short piece of yarn around any stitch to mark Rnd 1 as **right** side.
Rnd 2: Slip st in next dc and in first ch-1 sp, ch 3, (dc, ch 2, 2 dc) in same sp, work BPhdc around next 2 dc, work Shell in next ch-1 sp, † skip next dc, work BPhdc around next 4 dc, (work Shell in next ch-2 sp, skip next 3 dc, work BPhdc around next 4 dc) 24 times, work Shell in next ch-1 sp †, (work BPhdc around next 2 dc, work Shell in next ch-1 sp) twice, repeat from † to † once, work BPhdc around next 2 dc; join with slip st to top of beginning ch-3: 54 Shells.

Rnd 3: Slip st in next dc and in first ch-2 sp, ch 3, (dc, ch 2, 2 dc) in same sp, skip next 2 dc, work BPdc around each of next 2 BPhdc, work Shell in next ch-2 sp, † skip next 2 dc, work BPdc around each of next 4 BPhdc, work Shell in next ch-2 sp †, repeat from † to † 24 times **more**, (skip next 2 dc, work BPdc around each of next 2 BPhdc, work Shell in next ch-2 sp) twice, repeat from † to † 25 times, skip next 2 dc, work BPdc around each of next 2 BPhdc; join with slip st to top of beginning ch-3.
Rnd 4: Slip st in next dc and in first ch-2 sp, ch 1, sc in same sp, † (ch 3, sc) 3 times in same sp, ch 1, skip next 3 sts, (2 dc, ch 3, 2 dc) in next BPdc, ch 1, ★ (sc, ch 3, sc) in next ch-2 sp, ch 1, skip next 3 sts, (2 dc, ch 3, 2 dc) in next BPdc, ch 1; repeat from ★ 25 times **more** †, sc in next ch-2 sp, repeat from † to † once; join with slip st to first sc, finish off.

REMAINING 9 STRIPS
Work same as First Strip through Rnd 3.
Rnd 4 (Joining rnd): Slip st in next dc and in first ch-2 sp, ch 1, sc in same sp, (ch 3, sc) 3 times in same sp, ch 1, skip next 3 sts, (2 dc, ch 3, 2 dc) in next BPdc, ch 1, ★ (sc, ch 3, sc) in next ch-2 sp, ch 1, skip next 3 sts, (2 dc, ch 3, 2 dc) in next BPdc, ch 1; repeat from ★ 25 times **more**, sc in next ch-2 sp, (ch 3, sc) 3 times in same sp, ch 1, skip next 3 sts, (2 dc, ch 3, 2 dc) in next BPdc, ch 1, sc in next ch-2 sp, ch 1, holding Strips with **wrong** sides together, slip st in corresponding ch-3 sp on **previous Strip** *(Fig. 28, page 122)*, ch 1, sc in same sp on **new Strip**, ch 1, † skip next 3 sts, 2 dc in next BPdc, ch 1, slip st in next ch-3 sp on **previous Strip**, ch 1, 2 dc in same st on **new Strip**, ch 1, sc in next ch-2 sp, ch 1, slip st in next ch-3 sp on **previous Strip**, ch 1, sc in same sp on **new Strip**, ch 1 †, repeat from † to † 24 times **more**, skip next 3 sts, (2 dc, ch 3, 2 dc) in next BPdc, ch 1; join with slip st to first sc, finish off.

YESTERDAY'S DREAM

Worked in relaxing shades of blue and ecru, this breathtaking afghan is a lovely cover-up for an afternoon of daydreaming. Scalloped ends provide a soft touch.

Finished Size: 54" x 72"

MATERIALS

Worsted Weight Yarn:
Blue - 30½ ounces, (870 grams, 2,005 yards)
Lt Blue - 10 ounces, (280 grams, 655 yards)
Ecru - 10½ ounces, (300 grams, 690 yards)
Crochet hook, size J (6.00 mm) **or** size needed for gauge
Yarn needle

GAUGE: 13 dc and 8 rows = 4"
Each Strip = 3½" wide

STRIP (Make 15)
CENTER

To work **Cluster**, ★ YO, insert hook in st indicated, YO and pull up a loop, YO and draw through 2 loops on hook; repeat from ★ 2 times **more**, YO and draw through all 4 loops on hook **(Figs. 17a & b, page 120)**.
With Lt Blue, ch 203 **loosely**.
Foundation Row (Right side)**:** Work Cluster in fourth ch from hook, ★ ch 1, skip next ch, work Cluster in next ch; repeat from ★ across to last ch, dc in last ch; finish off: 100 Clusters and 99 ch-1 sps.
Note: Loop a short piece of yarn around last dc made to mark bottom edge and to mark Foundation Row as **right** side.

INNER TRIM
FIRST SIDE

With **right** side facing, join Blue with slip st in top of beginning ch; ch 1, sc in same st, place marker around last sc made for Border placement, skip first Cluster, 5 dc in next ch-1 sp, ★ skip next Cluster, sc in next ch-1 sp, skip next Cluster, 5 dc in next ch-1 sp; repeat from ★ across to last 2 sts, skip next Cluster, sc in last dc; finish off: 250 dc and 51 sc.

SECOND SIDE

With **right** side facing and working in free loops of beginning ch **(Fig. 31b, page 124)**, join Blue with slip st in first ch; ch 1, sc in same st, skip next ch; working around beginning ch, 5 dc in first ch-1 sp, ★ skip next ch, sc in next ch-1 sp, skip next ch, 5 dc in next ch-1 sp; repeat from ★ 48 times **more**, skip next ch, sc in next ch; finish off: 250 dc and 51 sc.

BORDER

With **right** side facing, join Ecru with slip st in marked sc; ch 3 **(counts as first dc, now and throughout)**, † place marker around last dc made for Outer Trim placement, 2 dc in same st, ★ skip next 2 dc, sc in next dc, skip next 2 dc, 3 dc in next sc; repeat from ★ across; working in end of rows, skip first row, (sc, 5 dc, sc) in next row (Foundation Row), skip next row †, dc in first sc, repeat from † to † once; join with slip st to first dc, finish off: 316 dc and 104 sc.

OUTER TRIM

With **right** side facing, join Blue with slip st in marked dc; ch 3, dc in next 2 dc, (dc in next sc and in next 3 dc) 50 times; finish off: 203 dc.
Repeat across opposite edge.

ASSEMBLY

Place two Strips together with **wrong** sides together and bottom edges at the same end. Using Blue and working through inside loops only, whipstitch Strips together, beginning in first dc of Outer Trim and ending in last dc of Outer Trim **(Fig. 33a, page 125)**.

Join remaining Strips in same manner, always working in same direction.

EDGING

With **right** side facing, join Blue with slip st in end of Outer Trim; ch 3, 2 dc in same row; working in sts of Border, sc in next sc, dc in next 2 dc, 3 dc in next dc, dc in next 2 dc, sc in next sc, 3 dc in end of next Outer Trim row, ★ sc in joining, 3 dc in end of next Outer Trim row; working in sts of Border, sc in next sc, dc in next 2 dc, 3 dc in next dc, dc in next 2 dc, sc in next sc, 3 dc in end of next Outer Trim row; repeat from ★ across; finish off. Repeat across opposite end.

VINTAGE FLOWER GARDEN

Reminiscent of a carefully plotted flower garden, this afghan features blooms made from scraps of pastel yarns. The sweet blossoms are worked on a chain that's \hidden behind green treble stitches.

Finished Size: 45¹/₂" x 63"

MATERIALS

Worsted Weight Yarn:
    Black - 23 ounces, (650 grams, 1,580 yards)
    Green - 16 ounces, (450 grams, 1,100 yards)
    Scraps - 6 ounces, (170 grams, 415 yards) **total**
      (We used 6 shades of yarn)
Crochet hook, size I (5.50 mm) **or** size needed for gauge
Yarn needle

GAUGE: Each Flower = 2¹/₄" (petal to petal)
           Each Strip = 3¹/₂" wide

STITCH GUIDE

JOINING DC
YO, insert hook in back ridge **(Fig. 26, page 122)** of center tr on petal indicated **and** in st or sp indicated, YO and pull up a loop, (YO and draw through 2 loops on hook) twice.
DOUBLE TREBLE CROCHET (abbreviated dtr)
YO 3 times, insert hook in st or sp indicated, YO and pull up a loop, (YO and draw through 2 loops on hook) 4 times **(Figs. 8a & b, page 117)**.
CLUSTER
YO twice, working in **front** and to **right** of next dtr, insert hook in ch-1 sp on rnd **below**, YO and pull up a loop, (YO and draw through 2 loops on hook) twice, YO twice, working in **front** and to **left** of same dtr, insert hook in **same** sp on rnd **below**, YO and pull up a loop, (YO and draw through 2 loops on hook) twice, YO and draw through all 3 loops on hook **(Figs. 17a & b, page 120)**.

STRIP A (Make 7)

Foundation Row: With desired color, ch 5, † 3 tr in top 2 strands of fifth ch from hook **(Fig. 2b, page 116)**, ch 4, slip st in same ch **(petal made)**, [ch 4, 3 tr in same ch, ch 4, slip st in same ch **(petal made)**] 3 times, holding working yarn between second and third petals, ch 1 **tightly** across center of petals, loop a short piece of yarn around any stitch to mark **right** side of Flower †, ★ ch 30 **more**, repeat from † to † once; repeat from ★ 6 times **more**; finish off: 8 Flowers (32 petals).

Rnd 1: With **right** side facing and working **behind** petals, join Green with slip st around ch across center of first Flower **(Fig. 24, page 122)**; ch 8 **(counts as first tr plus ch 4)**, (5 tr, ch 4, tr) in joining slip st, † ch 1, being careful not to twist Foundation Row, (5 tr, ch 1, 13 tr, ch 1, 5 tr) around ch between Flowers, ch 1, working **behind** petals, tr around ch across center of next Flower †, repeat from † to † 6 times **more**, ch 4, (5 tr, ch 4, tr) in base of tr just made, ch 1, working around ch between Flowers, tr **between** lower loops of next 5 tr **(Fig. 22, page 121)**, ch 1, tr **between** lower loops of next 13 tr, ch 1, tr **between** lower loops of next 5 tr, ch 1, ★ tr in base of corresponding tr on previous side, ch 1, tr **between** lower loops of next 5 tr, ch 1, tr **between** lower loops of next 13 tr, ch 1, tr **between** lower loops of next 5 tr, ch 1; repeat from ★ across; join with slip st to first tr, finish off.

Rnd 2: With **right** side facing, join Black with slip st in ch-4 sp to left of last joining; ch 3, work joining dc in next petal **and** in same ch-4 sp, (dc, ch 2, dc) in same sp, dc in next 2 tr, (dc, ch 1, dc) in next tr, dc in next 2 tr, (dc, ch 2, dc) in next ch-4 sp, work joining dc in next petal **and** in same ch-4 sp, dc in same sp, dc in next tr and in next ch-1 sp, † dc in next tr, work joining dc in next petal **and** in next tr, dc in next 3 tr, working in **front** of next ch-1 and in sp **before** next tr, dtr around ch between Flowers, dc in next 13 tr, working in **front** of next ch-1 and in sp **before** next tr, dtr around ch between Flowers, dc in next 3 tr, work joining dc in next petal **and** in next tr, (dc in next tr and in next ch-sp) twice †, repeat from † to † 6 times **more**, work joining dc in next petal **and** in same ch-4 sp, (dc, ch 2, dc) in same sp, dc in next 2 tr, (dc, ch 1, dc) in next tr, dc in next 2 tr, (dc, ch 2, dc) in next ch-4 sp, work joining dc in next petal **and** in same ch-4 sp, dc in same sp, dc in next tr and in next ch-1 sp, dc in next tr, work joining dc in next petal **and** in next tr, dc in next 3 tr, working around ch between Flowers and in **front** of next ch-1, dtr **between** lower loops of next dtr (on previous side), dc in next 13 tr, working in **front** of next ch-1, dtr **between** lower loops of next dtr, dc in next 3 tr, work joining dc in next petal **and** in next tr, dc in next tr, ★ (dc in next ch-1 sp and in next tr) twice, dc in next tr, work joining dc in next petal **and** in next tr, dc in next 3 tr, working in **front** of next ch-1, dtr **between** lower loops of next dtr, dc in next 13 tr, dtr **between** lower loops of next dtr, dc in next 3 tr, work joining dc in next petal **and** in next tr, dc in next tr; repeat from ★ 5 times **more**, dc in next ch-1 sp and in last tr; join with slip st to top of beginning ch-3.

Rnd 3: Ch 1, sc in same st and in next 2 dc, † ch 1, working in **front** of next ch-2, tr in sp **below** same chs, ch 1, sc in next 4 dc, ch 1, working in **front** of next ch-1, tr in st **below** same ch, ch 1, sc in next 4 dc, ch 1, working in **front** of next ch-2, tr in sp **below** same chs, ch 1, sc in next 10 dc, work Cluster, (sc in next 13 dc, work Cluster) 13 times †, sc in next 10 dc, repeat from † to † once, sc in last 7 dc; join with slip st to first sc, finish off.

STRIP B (Make 6)

Foundation Row: With desired color, ch 19, † 3 tr in fifth ch from hook, ch 4, slip st in same ch, (ch 4, 3 tr in same ch, ch 4, slip st in same ch) 3 times; holding working yarn between second and third petals, ch 1 **tightly** across center of petals †, mark **right** side of Flower, ★ ch 30 **more**, repeat from † to † once; repeat from ★ 5 times **more**, ch 14; finish off: 7 Flowers (28 petals).

Rnd 1: With **right** side facing, join Green with slip st in first ch; ch 4, (2 tr, ch 1, 5 tr, ch 1, 3 tr) in same ch, being careful not to twist Foundation Row, (6 tr, ch 1, 5 tr) around ch, ch 1, working **behind** petals, tr around ch across center of Flower, ch 1, † (5 tr, ch 1, 13 tr, ch 1, 5 tr) around ch between Flowers, ch 1, working **behind** petals, tr around ch across center next of Flower, ch 1 †, repeat from † to † 5 times **more**, holding ending ch-14, (5 tr, ch 1, 6 tr) around remaining ch, (3 tr, ch 1, 5 tr, ch 1, 3 tr) in last ch, working around ch, tr **between** lower loops of next 6 tr, ch 1, tr **between** lower loops of next 5 tr, ch 1, tr in base of corresponding tr on previous side, ch 1, tr **between** lower loops of next 5 tr, ch 1, ★ tr **between** lower loops of next 13 tr, ch 1, tr **between** lower loops of next 5 tr, ch 1, tr in base of corresponding tr on previous side, ch 1, tr **between** lower loops of next 5 tr, ch 1; repeat from ★ 5 times **more**, tr **between** lower loops of next 6 tr; join with slip st to top of beginning ch-4, finish off.

Rnd 2: With **right** side facing, join Black with slip st in same st as last joining; ch 3, dc in next 2 tr, (dc, ch 2, dc) in next ch-1 sp, dc in next 2 tr, (dc, ch 1, dc) in next tr, dc in next 2 tr, (dc, ch 2, dc) in next ch-1 sp, dc in next 9 tr, working in **front** of next ch-1 and in sp **before** next tr, dtr around ch between Flowers, dc in next 3 tr, work joining dc in next petal **and** in next tr, dc in next tr, (dc in next ch-1 sp and in next tr) twice, work joining dc in next petal **and** in next tr, dc in next 3 tr, working in **front** of next ch-1 and in sp **before** next tr, dtr around ch between Flowers, † dc in next 13 tr, working in **front** of next ch-1 and in sp **before** next tr, dtr around ch between Flowers, dc in next 3 tr, work joining dc in next petal **and** in next tr, dc in next tr, (dc in next ch-1 sp and in next tr) twice, work joining dc in next petal **and** in next tr, dc in next 3 tr, working in **front** of next ch-1 and in sp **before** next tr, dtr around ch between Flowers †, repeat from † to † 5 times **more**, dc in next 9 tr, (dc, ch 2, dc) in next ch-1 sp, dc in next 2 tr, (dc, ch 1, dc) in next tr, dc in next 2 tr, (dc, ch 2, dc) in next ch-1 sp, dc in next 9 tr, working in **front** of next ch-1, dtr **between** loops of next dtr (on previous side), dc in next 3 tr, work joining dc in next petal **and** in next tr, dc in next tr, (dc in next ch-1 sp and in next tr) twice, work joining dc in next petal **and** in next tr, dc in next 3 tr, working in **front** of next ch-1, dtr **between** lower loops of next dtr, ★ dc in next 13 tr, working in **front** of next ch-1,

dtr **between** lower loops of next dtr, dc in next 3 tr, work joining dc in next petal **and** in next tr, dc in next tr, (dc in next ch-1 sp and in next tr) twice, work joining dc in next petal **and** in next tr, dc in next 3 tr, working in **front** of next ch-1, dtr **between** lower loops of next dtr; repeat from ★ 5 times **more**, dc in last 6 tr; join with slip st to top of beginning ch-4, finish off.

Rnd 3: Ch 1, sc in same st and in next 3 dc, † ch 1, working in **front** of next ch-2, tr in sp **below** same chs, ch 1, sc in next 4 dc, ch 1, working in **front** of next ch-1, tr in st **below** same ch, ch 1, sc in next 4 dc, ch 1, working in **front** of next ch-2, tr in sp **below** same chs, ch 1, sc in next 10 dc, work Cluster, (sc in next 13 dc, work Cluster) 13 times †, sc in next 10 dc, repeat from † to † once, sc in last 6 dc; join with slip st to first sc, finish off.

ASSEMBLY

Note: Lay out Strips beginning with Strip A and alternating Strips A and B throughout.
Place two Strips with **wrong** sides together. Using Black and working through both loops, whipstitch Strips together, beginning in first corner tr and ending in next corner tr *(Fig. 33b, page 125)*.

Join remaining Strips in same manner, always working in same direction.

RESTFUL RAINBOW

A rainbow of soothing colors, this afghan offers a restful indulgence. Rows of double crochets in soft hues are enhanced with white trebles that extend from the border.

Finished Size: 45" x 60"

MATERIALS
Worsted Weight Yarn:
White - 21 ounces, (600 grams, 1,380 yards)
Scraps - 21 ounces, (600 grams, 1,380 yards) **total**
(We used 6 shades of pastels)
Crochet hook, size I (5.50 mm) **or** size needed for gauge
Yarn needle

GAUGE: Center = 1³/₄" wide and 7 rows = 4"
Each Strip = 2¹/₂" wide

STRIP (Make 18)
CENTER
With desired color, ch 8 **loosely**.

Row 1 (Right side)**:** Dc in fourth ch from hook and in each ch across: 6 sts.
Note: Loop a short piece of yarn around any stitch to mark Row 1 as **right** side and bottom edge.
Rows 2-103: Ch 3 **(counts as first dc, now and throughout)**, turn; dc in each st across: 6 dc.
Finish off.

BORDER
With **right** side facing and working in end of rows, join White with slip st in last row; ch 3, 2 dc in same sp, (working in **front** of first 2 dc on next row, tr around third dc, 3 dc in next row) across, working in free loops of beginning ch *(Fig. 31b, page 124)*, skip first 2 chs, 4 tr in each of next 2 chs; working in end of rows, 3 dc in first row, (working in **front** of first 2 dc on next row, tr around third dc, 3 dc in next row) across, skip first 2 dc on last row, 4 tr in each of next 2 dc; join with slip st to first dc, finish off: 118 tr.

ASSEMBLY

Place two Strips with **wrong** sides together and bottom edges at the same end. Using White and working through inside loops only, whipstitch Strips together, beginning in center dc of first 3-dc group and ending in center dc of last 3-dc group *(Fig. 33a, page 125)*.

Join remaining Strips in same manner, always working in same direction.

GENERAL INSTRUCTIONS

BASIC INFORMATION

YARN

Yarn weight (type or size) is divided into four basic categories:

Fingering (baby clothes), **Sport** (light-weight sweaters and afghans), **Worsted** (sweaters, afghans, toys), and **Bulky** (heavy sweaters, pot holders, and afghans).

Baby yarn may be classified as either Fingering or Sport — check the label for the recommended gauge.

These weights have absolutely nothing to do with the number of plies. Ply refers to the number of strands that have been twisted together to make the yarn. There are fingering weight yarns consisting of four plies, and there are bulky weight yarns made of a single ply.

Yarn listed under Materials for each afghan in this book is given in a generic weight. Once you know the weight of the yarn, any brand of the same weight may be used. This enables you to purchase the brand of yarn you like best. You may wish to purchase a single skein first and crochet a gauge swatch. Compare the way your yarn looks to the photograph to be sure that you will be satisfied with the results. How many skeins to buy depends on the yardage. Ounces and grams will vary from one brand of the same weight to another, but the yardage required will always remain the same provided gauge is met and maintained.

DYE LOTS

Yarn is dyed in large batches. Each batch is referred to as a "dye lot" and is assigned a number which will be listed on the yarn label. The color will vary slightly in shade from one dye lot to another. This color variance may be noticeable if skeins of yarn from different dye lots are used together in the same project.

So, when purchasing more than one skein of yarn for a particular color in your project, be sure to select skeins of yarn labeled with **identical** dye lot numbers. It is a good practice to purchase an extra skein to be sure that you have enough to complete your project.

TIPS FOR PURCHASING YARN

1. Always purchase the same weight yarn as specified in your project instructions.

2. It is best to refer to the yardage to determine how many skeins to purchase, since the number of yards per ounce may vary from one brand to another.

3. For each color in your project, purchase skeins in the same dye lot at one time, or you may risk being unable to find the same dye lot again.

4. If you are unsure if you will have enough yarn, buy an extra skein. Some stores will allow you to return unused skeins. Ask your local yarn shop about their return policy.

HOOKS

Crochet hooks used for working with **yarn** are made from aluminum, plastic, bone, or wood. They are lettered in sizes ranging from size B (2.25 mm) to the largest size Q (15.00 mm).

GAUGE

Gauge is the number of stitches and rows or rounds per inch and is used to determine the finished size of a project. All crochet patterns will specify the gauge that you must match to ensure proper size and to be sure you have enough yarn to complete the project.

Hook size given in instructions is merely a guide. Because everyone crochets differently — loosely, tightly, or somewhere in between — the finished size can vary, even when crocheters use the very same pattern, yarn, and hook.

Before beginning any crocheted item, it is absolutely necessary for you to crochet a gauge swatch in the pattern stitch indicated and with the weight of yarn and hook size suggested. Your swatch must be large enough to measure your gauge. Lay your swatch on a hard, smooth, flat surface. Then measure it, counting your stitches and rows or rounds carefully. If your swatch is smaller than specified or you have too many stitches per inch, try again with a larger size hook; if your swatch is larger or you don't have enough stitches per inch, try again with a smaller size hook. Keep trying until you find the size that will give you the specified gauge. DO NOT HESITATE TO CHANGE HOOK SIZE TO OBTAIN CORRECT GAUGE. Once proper gauge is obtained, measure width of piece approximately every 3" to be sure gauge remains consistent.

ABBREVIATIONS

BLO	Back Loop(s) Only
BPdc	Back Post double crochet(s)
BPhdc	Back Post half double crochet(s)
BPtr	Back Post treble crochet(s)
ch(s)	chain(s)
dc	double crochet(s)
dtr	double treble crochet(s)
FPdc	Front Post double crochet(s)
FPdtr	Front Post double treble crochet
FPhdc	Front Post half double crochet(s)
FPtr	Front Post treble crochet(s)
hdc	half double crochet(s)
mm	millimeters
Rnd(s)	Round(s)
sc	single crochet(s)
sp(s)	space(s)
st(s)	stitch(es)
tr	treble crochet(s)
YO	yarn over

★ — work instructions following ★ as many **more** times as indicated in addition to the first time.

† to † — work all instructions from first † to second † **as many** times as specified.

( ) or [ ] — work enclosed instructions **as many** times as specified by the number immediately following **or** work all enclosed instructions in the stitch or space indicated **or** contains explanatory remarks.

TERMS

chain loosely — work the chain **only** loose enough for the hook to pass through the chain easily when working the next row or round into the chain.

multiple — the number of stitches required to complete one repeat of a pattern.

post — the vertical shaft of a stitch.

right side vs. wrong side — the **right** side of your work is the side that will show when the piece is finished.

work across or around — continue working in the established pattern.

BASIC STITCH GUIDE

CHAIN

To work a chain stitch, begin with a slip knot on the hook. Bring the yarn **over** hook from **back** to **front**, catching the yarn with the hook and turning the hook slightly toward you to keep the yarn from slipping off. Draw the yarn through the slip knot *(Fig. 1)* (chain made, *abbreviated ch*).

Fig. 1

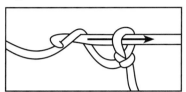

WORKING INTO THE CHAIN

When beginning a row of crochet in a chain, always skip the first chain from the hook, and work into the second chain from hook (for single crochet) or third chain from hook (for half double crochet), etc. *(Fig. 2a)*.

Fig. 2a

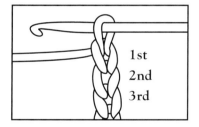

1st
2nd
3rd

Method 1: Insert hook under top two strands of each chain *(Fig. 2b)*.
Method 2: Insert hook into back ridge of each chain *(Fig. 2c)*.

Fig. 2b

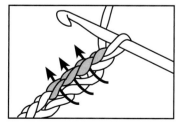

Fig. 2c

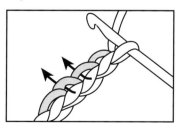

SLIP STITCH

This stitch is used to attach new yarn, to join work, or to move the yarn across a group of stitches without adding height. Insert hook in stitch or space indicated, YO and draw through stitch **and** loop on hook *(Fig. 3)* (slip stitch made, *abbreviated slip st*).

Fig. 3

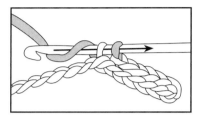

SINGLE CROCHET

Insert hook in stitch or space indicated, YO and pull up a loop (2 loops on hook), YO and draw through both loops on hook *(Fig. 4)* (single crochet made, *abbreviated sc*).

Fig. 4

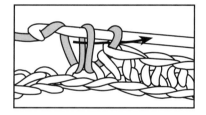

HALF DOUBLE CROCHET

YO, insert hook in stitch or space indicated, YO and pull up a loop (3 loops on hook), YO and draw through all 3 loops on hook *(Fig. 5)* (half double crochet made, *abbreviated hdc*).

Fig. 5

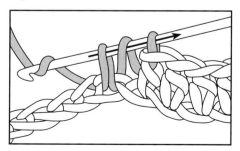

DOUBLE CROCHET

YO, insert hook in stitch or space indicated, YO and pull up a loop (3 loops on hook), YO and draw through 2 loops on hook *(Fig. 6a)*, YO and draw through remaining 2 loops on hook *(Fig. 6b)* (double crochet made, *abbreviated dc*).

Fig. 6a

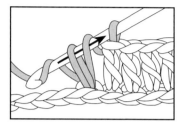

Fig. 6b

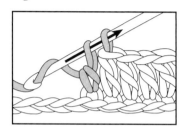

TREBLE CROCHET

YO twice, insert hook in stitch or space indicated, YO and pull up a loop (4 loops on hook) *(Fig. 7a)*, (YO and draw through 2 loops on hook) 3 times *(Fig. 7b)* (treble crochet made, *abbreviated tr)*.

Fig. 7a

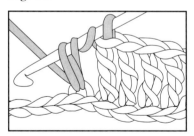

Fig. 7b

DOUBLE TREBLE CROCHET

YO 3 times, insert hook in stitch or space indicated, YO and pull up a loop (5 loops on hook) *(Fig. 8a)*, (YO and draw through 2 loops on hook) 4 times *(Fig. 8b)* (double treble crochet made, *abbreviated dtr)*.

Fig. 8a

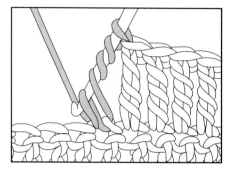

Fig. 8b

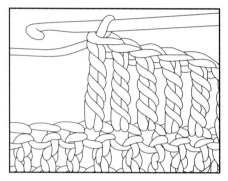

PATTERN STITCHES

POST STITCH

Work around post of stitch indicated, inserting hook in direction of arrow *(Fig. 9)*.

Fig. 9

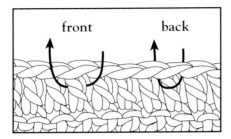

FRONT POST HALF DOUBLE CROCHET

YO, insert hook from **front** to **back** around post of stitch indicated *(Fig. 9)*, YO and pull up a loop (3 loops on hook) *(Fig. 10)*, YO and draw through all 3 loops on hook **(Front Post half double crochet made, abbreviated FPhdc)**.

Fig. 10

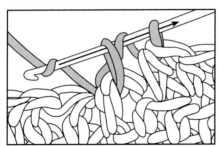

FRONT POST DOUBLE CROCHET

YO, insert hook from **front** to **back** around post of stitch indicated *(Fig. 9)*, YO and pull up a loop (3 loops on hook) *(Fig. 11)*, (YO and draw through 2 loops on hook) twice **(Front Post double crochet made, abbreviated FPdc)**.

Fig. 11

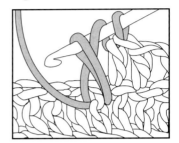

FRONT POST TREBLE CROCHET

YO twice, insert hook from **front** to **back** around post of stitch indicated *(Fig. 9)*, YO and pull up a loop (4 loops on hook) *(Fig. 12)*, (YO and draw through 2 loops on hook) 3 times **(Front Post treble crochet made, abbreviated FPtr)**.

Fig. 12

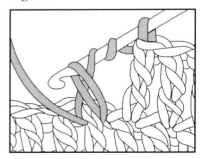

FRONT POST DOUBLE TREBLE CROCHET

YO 3 times, insert hook from **front** to **back** around post of stitch indicated (*Fig. 9, page 118*), YO and pull up a loop (5 loops on hook) (*Fig. 13*), (YO and draw through 2 loops on hook) 4 times (**Front Post double treble crochet made,** *abbreviated FPdtr*).

Fig. 13

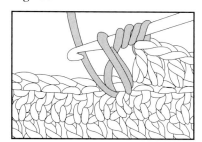

BACK POST HALF DOUBLE CROCHET

YO, insert hook from **back** to **front** around post of stitch indicated (*Fig. 9, page 118*), YO and pull up a loop (3 loops on hook) (*Fig. 14*), YO and draw through all 3 loops on hook (**Back Post half double crochet made,** *abbreviated BPhdc*).

Fig. 14

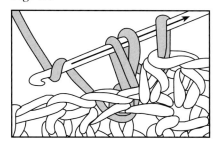

BACK POST DOUBLE CROCHET

YO, insert hook from **back** to **front** around post of stitch indicated (*Fig. 9, page 118*), YO and pull up a loop (3 loops on hook) (*Fig. 15*), (YO and draw through 2 loops on hook) twice (**Back Post double crochet made,** *abbreviated BPdc*).

Fig. 15

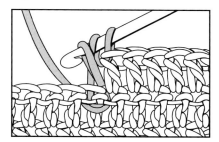

BACK POST TREBLE CROCHET

YO twice, insert hook from **back** to **front** around post of stitch indicated (*Fig. 9, page 118*), YO and pull up a loop (4 loops on hook) (*Fig. 16*), (YO and draw through 2 loops on hook) 3 times (**Back Post treble crochet made,** *abbreviated BPtr*).

Fig. 16

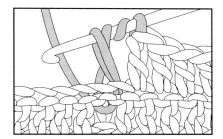

CLUSTER

A Cluster can be worked all in the same stitch or space *(Figs. 17a & b)*, **or** across several stitches *(Figs. 17c & d)*.

Fig. 17a

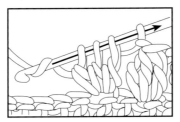

Fig. 17b

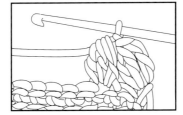

Fig. 17c

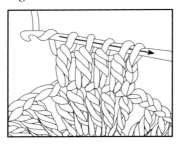

Fig. 17d

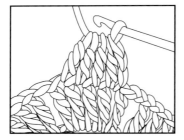

DTR CLUSTER

YO 3 times, working in end of rows of Center, insert hook in same sp and to **right** of 3-dc on Rnd 1 **below** last 3 sc made *(Fig. 18a)*, YO and pull up a loop, (YO and draw through 2 loops on hook) 3 times, YO 3 times, skip next 6 dc on Rnd 1, insert hook in same sp and to **left** of last skipped dc *(Fig. 18b)*, YO and pull up a loop, (YO and draw through 2 loops on hook) 3 times, YO and draw through all 3 loops on hook. Do **not** skip st behind dtr Cluster.

Fig. 18a

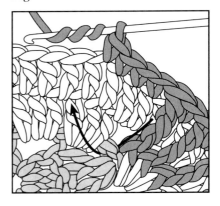

Fig. 18b

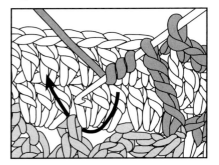

POPCORN

Work 5 dc in stitch or space indicated, drop loop from hook, insert hook in first dc of 5-dc group, hook dropped loop and draw through (**Fig. 19**).

Fig. 19

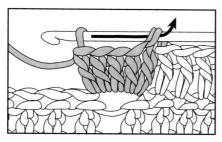

PUFF STITCH

★ YO, insert hook in st or sp indicated, YO and pull up a loop even with loop on hook; repeat from ★ 3 times **more**, YO and draw through all 9 loops on hook (**Fig. 20**).

Fig. 20

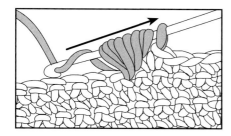

DECREASE

Insert hook from **front** to **back** in next dc, skip next dc and insert hook from **back** to **front** in next dc (**Fig. 21**), YO and pull up a loop, YO and draw through both loops on hook.

Fig. 21

WORKING BETWEEN LOWER LOOPS

Insert hook **between** lower loops of stitch on opposite side of chain (**Fig. 22**).

Fig. 22

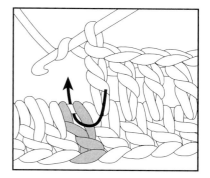

WORKING AROUND END OF DC-GROUP

Dtr around end of 5-dc group indicated on Center (**Fig. 23**).

Fig. 23

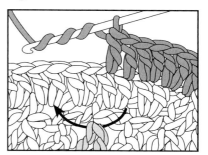

WORKING ACROSS CENTER OF FLOWER

Slip st around ch across center of Flower *(Fig. 24)*.

Fig. 24

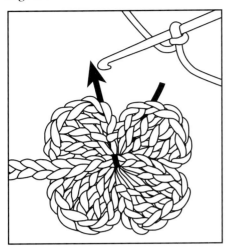

WORKING IN PREVIOUS CH-3 SP

Slip st in last ch-3 sp made *(Fig. 25)*.

Fig. 25

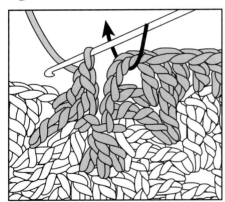

JOINING DOUBLE CROCHET

YO, insert hook in back ridge *(Fig. 26)* of stitch indicated and in stitch or space indicated, YO and pull up a loop, (YO and draw through 2 loops on hook) twice **(joining double crochet made,** *abbreviated joining dc)*.

Fig. 26

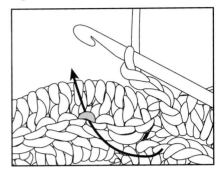

WORKING BETWEEN STITCHES

When insructed to work in space **before** a stitch or in spaces **between** stitches, insert hook in space indicated by arrow *(Fig. 27)*.

Fig. 27

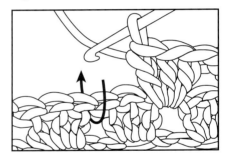

NO SEW JOINING

Hold Strips with **wrong** sides together. Slip stitch into stitch or space indicated *(Fig. 28)*.

Fig. 28

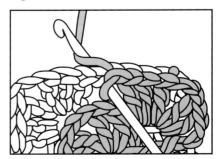

STITCHING TIPS

WEAVING IN YARN ENDS

Good finishing techniques make a big difference in the quality of any crocheted piece. Make a habit of taking care of loose ends as you work. **Never** tie a knot in your yarn. They may poke through to the right side and will sometimes come untied and unravel. Weaving in the ends gives a much better result. Thread a yarn needle with the yarn end. With **wrong** side facing, weave the needle through several stitches, then reverse the direction and weave it back through several more stitches. When the end is secure, clip the yarn off close to your work.
You may also hide your ends as you work by crocheting over them for several inches to secure, then weave in opposite direction; clip the remaining lengths off close to your work.
Always check your work to be sure the yarn ends do not show on the right side.

EDGING
SINGLE CROCHET EVENLY ACROSS OR AROUND

When instructed to single crochet evenly across or around, the single crochets should be spaced to keep the piece lying flat. Work a few single crochets at a time, checking periodically to be sure your edge is not distorted. If the edge is puckering, you need to add a few more single crochets; if the edge is ruffling, you need to remove some single crochets. Keep trying until the edge lies smooth and flat.

HOW TO DETERMINE THE RIGHT SIDE

Many designs are made with the **front** of the stitch as the **right** side. Notice that the **fronts** of the stitches are smooth *(Fig. 29a)* and the **backs** of the stitches are bumpy *(Fig. 29b)*. For easy identification, it may be helpful to loop a short piece of yarn around any stitch to mark **right** side.

Fig. 29a

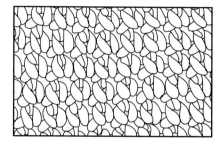

Fig. 29b

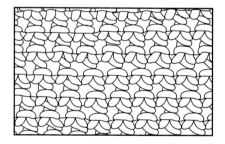

JOINING WITH SC

When instructed to join with sc, begin with a slip knot on hook. Insert hook in stitch or space indicated, YO and pull up a loop, YO and draw through both loops on hook.

CHANGING COLORS

Work the last stitch to within one step of completion, hook new yarn *(Fig. 30a)* and draw through all loops on hook. Cut old yarn and work over both ends. When working in rounds, drop old yarn and join with slip stitch to first stitch using new yarn *(Fig. 30b)*.

Fig. 30a

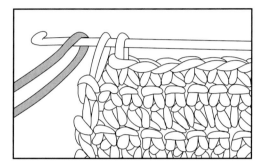

Fig. 30b

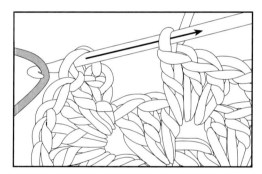

FREE LOOPS

After working in Back Loops Only on a row or round, there will be a ridge of unused loops. These are called the free loops. Later, when instructed to work in the free loops of same row or round, work in these loops *(Fig. 31a)*. When instructed to work in free loops of a beginning chain, work in loop indicated by arrow *(Fig. 31b)*.

Fig. 31a

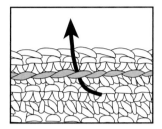

Fig. 31b

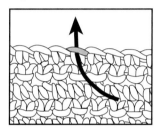

BACK OR FRONT LOOP ONLY

Work only in loop(s) indicated by arrow *(Fig. 32)*.

Fig. 32

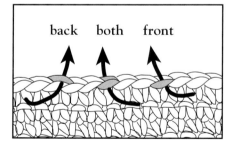

FINISHING

WASHING AND BLOCKING

Blocking "sets" a crocheted item and smooths the stitches to give your work a professional appearance. Before blocking, check the yarn label for any special instructions because many acrylics and some blends can be damaged during blocking.

Note: Always use stainless steel pins.

Thread projects should be washed before blocking. Using a mild detergent and warm water, gently squeeze suds through the piece, being careful not to rub, twist, or wring. Rinse several times in cool, clear water. Roll piece in a clean terry towel and gently press out the excess moisture. Lay piece on a flat surface and shape to proper size; where needed, pin in place. Allow to dry **completely**. Doilies can be spray starched for extra crispness.

On fragile **acrylics** that can be blocked, pin the item to the correct size on a towel-covered board, and cover the item with dampened bath towels. When the towels are dry, the item is blocked.

If the item is **hand washable**, carefully launder it using a mild soap or detergent. Rinse it without wringing or twisting. Remove any excess moisture by rolling it in a succession of dry towels. If you prefer, you may put it in the final spin cycle of your washer - but do not use water. Lay the item on a large towel on a flat surface out of direct sunlight. Gently smooth and pat it to the desired size and shape, comparing the measurements to the pattern instructions as necessary. When the item is completely dry, it is blocked.

Steaming is an excellent method of blocking crochet items, especially those made with **wool or wool blends**. Turn the item wrong side out and pin it to the correct size on a board covered with towels. Hold a steam iron or steamer just above the item and steam it thoroughly. Never let the weight of the iron touch your item because it will flatten the stitches. Leave the garment pinned until it is completely dry.

SEAMS

A tapestry or yarn needle is best to use for sewing seams because the blunt point is less likely to split the yarn. Use the same yarn the item was made with to sew the seams. However, if the yarn is textured or bulky, it may be easier to sew the seam with a small, smooth yarn of the same color, such as tapestry yarn or an acrylic needlepoint yarn. If a different yarn is used for the seams, be sure the care instructions for both yarns are the same. If the yarn used to crochet the item is machine washable, the seam yarn must also be machine washable.

WHIPSTITCH

With **wrong** sides together and beginning in corner stitch, sew through both pieces once to secure the beginning of the seam, leaving an ample yarn end to weave in later. Insert the needle from **right** to **left** through **inside** loops of each piece *(Fig. 33a)* or through **both** loops *(Fig. 33b)*. Bring the needle around and insert it from **right** to **left** through the next loops of **both** pieces. Repeat along the edge, keeping the sewing yarn fairly loose and being careful to match stitches.

Fig. 33a

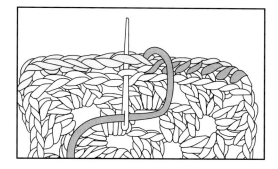

Fig. 33b

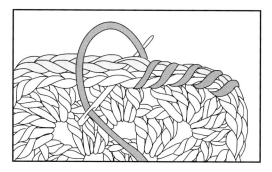

FRINGE

Cut a piece of cardboard 3" wide and 1/2" longer than desired fringe. Wind the yarn **loosely** and **evenly** around the cardboard until the card is filled, then cut across one end; repeat as needed.

Align the number of strands desired and fold in half. With **wrong** side facing and using a crochet hook, draw the folded end up through a stitch or row and pull the loose ends through the folded end *(Fig. 34a)*; draw the knot up **tightly** *(Fig. 34b)*. Repeat, spacing as desired. Lay flat on a hard surface and trim the ends.

Fig. 34a

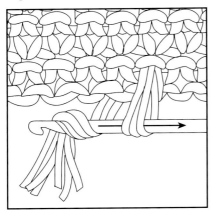

Fig. 34b

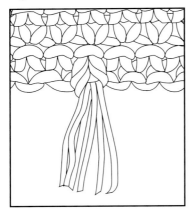

TASSEL

Cut a piece of cardboard 3" wide and as long as you want your finished tassel to be. Wind a double strand of yarn around the cardboard approximately 12 times. Cut an 18" length of yarn and insert it under all of the strands at the top of the cardboard; pull up **tightly** and tie securely. Leave the yarn ends long enough to attach the tassel. Cut the yarn at the opposite end of the cardboard and then remove it *(Fig. 35a)*. Cut a 6" length of yarn and wrap it **tightly** around the tassel twice, 1" below the top *(Fig. 35b)*; tie securely. Trim the ends.

Fig. 35a

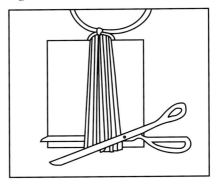

Fig. 35b

CREDITS

We extend a warm *thank you* to the generous people who allowed us to photograph our afghans at their homes and places of business.

To Magna IV Color Imaging of Little Rock, Arkansas, we say thank you for the superb color reproduction and excellent pre-press preparation.

We want to especially thank photographers Ken West, Larry Pennington, Mark Mathews, and Karen Shirey of Peerless Photography, Little Rock, Arkansas, and Jerry R. Davis of Jerry Davis Photography, Little Rock, Arkansas, for their time, patience, and excellent work.

We would like to extend a special word of thanks to the talented designers who created the lovely projects in this book:

Alexander-Stratton: *Formal Garden*, page 24; *Nostalgic Cover-up*, page 32; *Popcorn Braid*, page 54; and *Tasseled Ribbons*, page 56

Jennie Black: *Blueberry Cobbler*, page 72

Judy Bolin: *Peach Orchard*, page 26, and *Fringed Fancy*, page 28

Dorris Brooks: *Gemstone Cables*, page 70

Rose Marie Brooks: *Braids for Baby*, page 104

Carolyn Christmas: *Little Girl's Fancy*, page 52

Anne Halliday: *Sunny Scallops*, page 48

Jan Hatfield: *Rustic Lap Robe*, page 6; *Peachy Trellis*, page 10; *Ruffled Treasure*, page 18; *Truly Victorian*, page 22; *Easygoing Afghan*, page 30; *Butterfly Blues*, page 38; *Around We Go!*, page 40; *Aztec Touch*, page 42; *Basketweave Beauty*, page 66; *Spring Carnival*, page 76; *Ropes of Jade*, page 80; *Cozy Cover-up*, page 82; *Pretty Posts*, page 86; *Cloud-Soft Shells*, page 92; *Gentleman's Choice*, page 98; *Summer Sherbet*, page 100; *Trailing Diamonds*, page 102; *Yesterday's Dream*, page 108; and *Restful Rainbow*, page 112

Lucia Karge: *Rosy Ribbons*, page 8

Valesha Marshell Kirksey: *Country Sprinkles*, page 64; *Rubies & Pearls*, page 74; *Handsome Classic*, page 94; and *Vintage Flower Garden*, page 110

Jennine Korejko: *Snowy Lullaby* and *Blue & White Bliss*, page 14; *Cuddly Clusters*, page 20; *Filigree Fantasy*, page 34; *Crowning Beauty*, page 36; *Timeless Tapestry*, page 58; *Lavish Texture*, page 88; *Terrific Twists*, page 96; and *Fanciful Sculpture*, page 106

Patricia Kristoffersen: *Early-American Spirit*, page 46; *Majestic Miles*, page 78; and *Teatime Elegance*, page 90

Melissa Leapman: *Cinnamon Sticks*, page 16

Kay Meadors: *Fanciful Flowers*, page 12; *Holly Garland*, page 50; *Arrowhead Valley*, page 60; and *Christmas Wreaths*, page 62

Frances Moore-Kyle: *Black Tie-White Tie*, page 44

Debra Nettles: *All-Around Wrap*, page 68

Rhonda Semonis: *Queen Anne's Lace*, page 4

Brenda Stratton: *Sentimental Shells*, page 84

We extend a sincere *thank you* to the people who assisted in making and testing many of the projects in this book: Janet Akins, Lissa Ammann, Belinda Baxter, Jeanne Bennett, Pam Bland, Delois Bynum, Mike Cates, Lee Ellis, Naomi Greening, Raymelle Greening, Kathleen Hardy, Chrys Harvey, Lisa Hightower, Connie Hilton, Vicki Kellogg, Cheryl Knepper, Liz Lane, Carla Rains, Hilda Rivero, Rondi Rowell, Faith Stewart, Clare Stringer, Margaret Taverner, Carol Thompson, Mary Valen, and Augustine Zajac.